HIGH FAT LOW CARB VEGAN COOKBOOK

Discover the Plant Based Diet Path To Enhanced Weight Loss And Better Health With This Ultimate Combination Cookbook

SOFIA KENNEDY

Copyright © 2020 Sofia Kennedy

All Rights Reserved

Copyright 2020 By Sofia Kennedy - All rights reserved.

The following book is produced below with the goal of providing information that is as accurate and reliable as possible. Regardless, purchasing this eBook can be seen as consent to the fact that both the publisher and the author of this book are in no way experts on the topics discussed within and that any recommendations or suggestions that are made herein are for entertainment purposes only. Professionals should be consulted as needed prior to undertaking any of the action endorsed herein.

This declaration is deemed fair and valid by both the American Bar Association and the Committee of Publishers Association and is legally binding throughout the United States.

Furthermore, the transmission, duplication or reproduction of any of the following work including specific information will be considered an illegal act irrespective of if it is done electronically or in print. This extends to creating a secondary or tertiary copy of the work or a recorded copy and is only allowed with express written consent from the Publisher. All additional right reserved.

The information in the following pages is broadly considered to be a truthful and accurate account of facts and as such any inattention, use or misuse of the information in question by the reader will render any resulting actions solely under their purview. There are no scenarios in which the publisher or the original author of this work can be in any fashion deemed liable for any hardship or damages that may befall them after undertaking information described herein.

Additionally, the information in the following pages is intended only for informational purposes and should thus be thought of as universal. As befitting its nature, it is presented without assurance regarding its prolonged validity or interim quality. Trademarks that are mentioned are done without written consent and can in no way be considered an endorsement from the trademark holder.

Table of Contents

PART I 11

Vegan Cookbook 12

    Chapter 1: Breakfast Recipes 15

        Shamrock Sandwich 15

        Breakfast Burrito 17

        Gingerbread Waffles 19

        Green Chickpeas And Toast 21

        Asparagus And Tomato Quiche 22

        Breakfast Bowl 24

        Tofu Pancakes 26

    Chapter 2: Side Dish Recipes 28

        Baked Beans 28

        Baked Potato Wedges 30

        Black Beans And Quinoa 31

        Roasted Lemon Garlic Broccoli 32

        Spicy Tofu 33

        Spanish Rice 34

        Pepper And Lemon Pasta 35

    Chapter 3: High Protein Recipes 36

        Kale Salad With Spicy Tempeh Bits And Chickpeas 36

        Protein Bars 39

        Tofu And Spinach Scramble 41

        Vegan Tacos 42

        Grilled Tofu Steaks And Spinach Salad 44

Corn, Quinoa, And Edamame Salad 46

Lentil Soup 48

Chapter 4: Dessert Recipes 50

Chocolate Pudding 50

Orange Cake 52

Pumpkin Tofu Pie 54

Vegan Brownie 56

Vegan Cupcake 57

Vanilla Cake 59

Miracle Fudge 61

Chapter 5: Sauces & Dips Recipes 62

Tomato Jam 62

Walnut Kale Pesto 63

Ranch Dressing 64

PART II 65

Vegan Keto 66

Chapter 1: Breakfast Recipes 68

Tofu Scramble 68

Low Carb Pancakes 70

Cauliflower Hashbrowns 72

Vanilla Waffles 73

Pecan And Cinnamon Porridge 74

Chapter 2: Appetizers Recipes 75

Arugula Salad 76

Cauliflower Soup 78

Cauliflower Zucchini Fritters 80

Zucchini Noodles And Avocado Sauce 81

    Roasted Brussels Sprouts 83

Chapter 3: Main Course Recipes 84

    Mushroom Tomato Spaghetti Squash 84

    Vegan Shakshuka 86

    Zucchini Lasagna 87

    Arugula Tomato And Avocado Salad 89

    Mushroom Fried Rice 91

Chapter 4: Snacks And Dessert Recipes 92

    Almond Flour Crackers 92

    Guacamole 94

    Strawberry And Avocado Ices 95

    Chocolate And Peanut Butter Ice Cream 97

    Carrot Cake 99

    Almond And Chocolate Pudding 101

PART III 102

Vegetarian Cookbook 103

Chapter 1: Breakfast Recipes 105

    Black Bean Bowl 106

    Coconut Blueberry Ricotta Bowl 108

    Broccoli Quiche 109

    Tomato Bagel Sandwich 111

    Cornmeal And Blueberry Pancakes 112

    Breakfast Tortilla 114

    Zucchini Frittata 115

    Oatmeal And Strawberry Smoothie 117

Chapter 2: Appetizers Recipes 119

    Buffalo Cauliflower 119

    Garlic Bread And Veggie Delight 121

    Spinach Parmesan Balls 123

    Cheese Garlic Bread 124

    Stuffed Mushrooms 125

    Tomato Bruschetta 127

    Spicy Pumpkin Seeds 128

Chapter 3: Soups & Side Dishes Recipes 129

    Carrot Soup 129

    Celery Soup 131

    Tomato Soup And Halloumi Croutons 133

    Baked Potatoes And Mushrooms With Spinach 135

    Garlic Potatoes 136

    Buttery Carrots 137

Chapter 4: Main Course Recipes 138

    Nut And Tofu Loaf 138

    Velvety Chickpea Curry 141

    Tofu Pad Thai 143

    Eggplant Parmesan 145

    Veg Korma 146

    Mac And Cheese 148

    Sesame Noodles 149

Chapter 5: Dessert Recipes 150

    Raspberry And Rosewater Sponge Cake 150

    Easy Tiramisu 153

    Chocolate Marquise 155

    Lemon Syllabub 157

PART IV **158**

Smoothie Diet Recipes 159

Chapter 1: Fruit Smoothies 160
Quick Fruit Smoothie 160
Triple Threat Smoothie 162
Tropical Smoothie 163
Fruit and Mint Smoothie 164
Banana Smoothie 166
Dragon Fruit Smoothie 168
Kefir Blueberry Smoothie 170
Ginger Fruit Smoothie 172
Fruit Batido 174
Banana Peanut Butter Smoothie 175

Chapter 2: Breakfast Smoothies 176
Berry Banana Smoothie 176
Berry Surprise 177
Coconut Matcha Smoothie 179
Cantaloupe Frenzy 180
Berry Lemon Smoothie 181
Orange Glorious 183
Grapefruit Smoothie 184
Sour Smoothie 185
Ginger Orange Smoothie 186
Cranberry Smoothie 187
Creamsicle Smoothie 189
Sunshine Smoothie 190

Chapter 3: Vegetable Smoothies 191
Mango Kale Berry Smoothie 191

Breakfast Pink Smoothie..192

Butternut Squash Smoothie..194

Zucchini and Wild Blueberry Smoothie 195

Cauliflower and Blueberry Smoothie 196

Immunity Booster Smoothie...197

Ginger, Carrot, and Turmeric Smoothie 199

Romaine Mango Smoothie 200

Fig Zucchini Smoothie..201

Carrot Peach Smoothie..202

Sweet Potato and Mango Smoothie..204

Carrot Cake Smoothie..205

Chapter 4: Green Smoothies..206

Kale Avocado Smoothie 206

Celery Pineapple Smoothie..208

Cucumber Mango and Lime Smoothie 209

Kale, Melon, and Broccoli Smoothie 211

Kiwi Spinach Smoothie 213

Avocado Smoothie 214

PART I

Vegan Cookbook

The vegan diet has gained immense popularity in the past few years. With an increasing number of participants, people have made up their mind to opt for the vegan options for health, environmental, or ethical reasons. When done in the perfect way, a vegan diet can help in showcasing a wide array of health benefits, for example, better control over blood sugar and a slimmer waistline. However, when a diet is based entirely on plant derivatives, it can result in a nutrient deficiency in various cases.

Veganism is being defined as a simple way of living that aims at excluding all major forms of animal cruelty and exploitation, whether for daily food, clothing, or some other purpose. For all these reasons, this diet does not include any form of animal products, such as eggs, dairy, and meat. It has been found that all those people who tend to practice veganism are thinner and also comes with a lower BMI or body mass index when compared with non-vegans. This can easily explain the primary reason why the majority of the people are turning to this form of diet as the only way for losing extra weight.

Adopting a vegan diet can help keep the blood sugar level under proper check and type 2 diabetes. According to some studies, vegans tend to benefit from the lower levels of blood sugar, higher sensitivity to insulin, and about 77% lower risk of developing diabetes than the non-vegans. The majority of the advantages can be easily explained by the increased consumption of fiber, which can blunt the blood sugar response. Several observational studies reported that vegans could have a 74% lower risk of having increased blood pressure along with a 43% lower risk of suffering from any chronic heart disease.

There is a specific food group that you will need to omit for following a vegan diet. This group of foods includes:

- **Poultry and meat:** Lamb, beef, veal, pork, organ meat, chicken, wild meat, goose, turkey, duck, etc.

- **Dairy:** Yogurt, butter, milk, cheese, ice cream, cream, etc.

- **Seafood and fish:** Fish of all types, squid, anchovies, calamari, shrimp, lobster, mussels, crab, etc.

- **Eggs:** From ostrich, chicken, fish, quail, etc.

- **Products from bees:** Bee pollen, honey, royal jelly, etc.

- **Ingredients based on animals:** Casein, whey, egg white albumen, shellac, lactose, gelatin, L-cysteine, isinglass, omega-3 fatty acids derived from fish, vitamin D3 derived from animals, and carmine.

You can opt for alternatives such as legumes, seitan, tofu, seeds, nut butter, nuts, veggies, fruits, whole grains, etc. The cooking style will remain the same, and the only difference will be the ingredients you are going to use.

Chapter 1: Breakfast Recipes

Breakfast is an essential meal of the day that needs to be fulfilled properly. Here are some vegan breakfast recipes for you.

Shamrock Sandwich

Total Prep & Cooking Time: Fifteen minutes

Yields: One serving

Nutrition Facts: Calories: 562 | Protein: 23g | Carbs: 43.2g | Fat: 31g | Fiber: 8.3g

Ingredients:

- One sausage patty (vegan)
- One cup of kale
- Two tsps. of olive oil (extra virgin)
- One tbsp. of pepitas
- Pepper and salt (according to taste)

For the sauce:

- One tbsp. of vegan mayonnaise
- One tsp. of jalapeno (chopped)
- One-fourth tsp. of paprika (smoky)

Other ingredients:

- One-fourth of an avocado (sliced)
- One toasted English muffin

Method:

1. Start by toasting the English muffin and keep it aside.

2. Take a sauté pan and drizzle some oil in it. Add the sausage patty and cook for two minutes on each side.

3. Add pepitas and kale to the hot pan. Add pepper and salt for adjusting the taste. When the kale gets soft, and the patty gets browned, remove the pan from heat.

4. Combine the spicy sauce.

5. Assemble the sandwich with sauce on the muffins and add the patty, avocado, pepitas, and kale.

Breakfast Burrito

Total Prep & Cooking Time: Thirty minutes

Yields: Two servings

Nutrition Facts: Calories: 618 | Protein: 20.3g | Carbs: 113g | Fat: 13.7g | Fiber: 21g

Ingredients:

- Three-fourth cup of rice (rinsed)
- Two cups of water
- One-fourth tsp. of salt
- One tbsp. of lime juice
- Half cup of cilantro (chopped)

For onions and hash browns:

- Half red onion
- Four red potatoes
- Two tbsp. of olive oil
- One-fourth tsp. of each
    - Black pepper (ground)
    - Salt

For black beans:

- One cup of black beans (cooked)
- One-fourth tsp. of each
    - Chili powder
    - Cumin powder
    - Garlic powder

For the avocado slaw:

- One avocado
- Two tbsps. of lime juice
- One cup of green cabbage (sliced thinly)
- One jalapeno (sliced)
- Half tsp. of each
    - Black pepper
    - Salt

For serving:

- Two flour tortillas
- Half avocado (ripe, sliced)
- One-fourth cup of salsa

Method:

1. Boil water, salt, and rice in a pan. Simmer the mixture for twenty minutes until the rice turns fluffy. Drain and keep aside.
2. Heat oil in a pan. Chop the potatoes into small pieces and slice the onions in rings. Add the potatoes along with the onions to the pan. Add pepper and salt for seasoning; toss the mixture for five minutes. Keep aside.
3. Prepare the beans in a saucepan over a medium flame.
4. For making the slaw, mix lime juice and avocado in a bowl. Mash the avocado and mix. Add jalapeno, cabbage, and toss for combining. Add pepper and salt for seasoning.
5. Add cilantro and lime juice to the rice and combine using a fork.
6. Warm the tortillas in a pan or microwave for twenty seconds.
7. Add the prepared fillings to the tortillas in order of your choice and top with salsa; add sliced avocado from the top. Roll the tortillas and slice in half.
8. Serve with extra black beans and potatoes by the side.

Gingerbread Waffles

Total Prep & Cooking Time: Fifteen minutes

Yields: Six servings

Nutrition Facts: Calories: 170 | Protein: 4.2g | Carbs: 27.3g | Fat: 4.7g | Fiber: 3.9g

Ingredients:

- One cup of flour
- One tbsp. of flax seeds (ground)

- Two tsps. of baking powder
- One-fourth tsp. of each
    - Salt
    - Baking soda
- One tsp. of cinnamon (ground)
- One and a half tsps. of ginger (ground)
- Four tbsps. of brown sugar
- One cup of any non-dairy milk
- Two tbsps. of apple cider vinegar
- Two tbsps. of molasses
- One and a half tbsps. of olive oil

Method:

1. Preheat a waffle iron and grease it.
2. Put the dry ingredients in a mixing bowl and combine well.
3. Combine the wet ingredients in a medium mixing bowl or jug. Mix well until properly combined.
4. Add the mixture of wet ingredients into the dry mixture and mix well. The batter needs to be thick. In case the batter is excessively thick, you can add two tbsps. of non-dairy milk to the batter and mix.
5. Pour the batter in batches in the waffle iron and cook until steam stops to come out from the sides.
6. Open the waffle iron and take out the waffle carefully.
7. Serve warm.

Green Chickpeas And Toast
Total Prep & Cooking Time: Thirty minutes

Yields: Two servings

Nutrition Facts: Calories: 189 | Protein: 11.3g | Carbs: 27.1g | Fat: 3.2g | Fiber: 9.3g

Ingredients:

- Two tbsps. of olive oil
- Three shallots (diced)
- One-fourth tsp. of paprika (smoked)
- Two cloves of garlic (diced)
- Half tsp. of each
    - Sweet paprika
    - Salt
    - Cinnamon
    - Sugar
- Black pepper (according to taste)
- Two tomatoes (skinned)
- Two cups of chickpeas (cooked)
- Four crusty bread slices

Method:

1. Take a medium pan and heat oil in it.

2. Add the diced shallots to the oil and stir-fry. Add garlic to the pan. Cook for five minutes until shallots turn translucent.

3. Add spices to the pan and combine well with garlic and shallots. Stir for two minutes.

4. Add the tomatoes to the pan and squash them using a spoon or spatula. Add four tbsps. of water to the pan and simmer for twelve minutes.

5. Add cooked chickpeas and mix well. Add pepper, sugar, and salt.

6. Serve the cooked chickpeas on bread slices.

Asparagus And Tomato Quiche

Total Prep & Cooking Time: One hour and twenty minutes

Yields: Eight servings

Nutrition Facts: Calories: 219 | Protein: 4.1g | Carbs: 20.6g | Fat: 11.7g | Fiber: 3g

Ingredients:

- Two cups of flour
- Half tsp. of salt
- Half cup of non-dairy butter
- Two tbsps. of water (ice cold)

For filling:

- One tbsp. of coconut oil
- One cup of asparagus (chopped)
- One-fourth cup of onion (minced)
- Three tbsps. of each
    - Sun-dried tomatoes (chopped)
    - Nutritional yeast
    - Basil (chopped)
- One block of tofu (firm)
- One tbsp. of each
    - Flour
    - Non-dairy milk
- One tsp. of each
    - Minced onion (dehydrated)
    - Mustard
- Two tsps. of lemon juice
- Half tsp. of each
    - Salt

- Turmeric
- Liquid smoke

Method:

1. Spray a pie pan with oil and keep aside. Preheat your oven at 180 degrees Celsius.

2. Mix salt along with flour in a bowl. Add non-dairy butter along with cold water to the flour. Knead the dough on a working surface.

3. Press the dough on the pan. Bake the dough in the preheated oven for ten minutes.

4. Heat some oil in a pan and start adding asparagus, tomato, and onion—Cook for three minutes.

5. Combine onion, tofu, yeast, flour, non-dairy milk, lemon juice, liquid smoke, and salt in a blender.

6. Combine the mixture of asparagus with the tofu mixture.

7. Add the filling on the baked crust and smoothen the top.

8. Bake for half an hour.

9. Serve warm.

Breakfast Bowl

Total Prep & Cooking Time: One hour and twenty-five minutes

Yields: Two servings

Nutrition Facts: Calories: 350 | Protein: 7.2g | Carbs: 54g | Fat: 11.3g | Fiber: 9.3g

Ingredients:

- Two small sweet potatoes
- Cinnamon (ground, according to taste)
- Two tbsps. of each
    - Chopped nuts
    - Raisins
    - Almond butter

Method:

1. Preheat your oven at 180/160 degrees Celsius. Wash the potatoes and dry them using a kitchen towel. Use a fork for poking holes in the potatoes and wrap them using aluminum foil. Bake the potatoes for eighty minutes. Allow the potatoes to cool down before peeling.

2. Peel the baked potatoes and mash them with cinnamon.

3. Top with chopped nuts and raisins. Drizzle some almond butter from the top and serve.

Tofu Pancakes

Total Prep & Cooking Time: Twenty minutes

Yields: Six servings

Nutrition Facts: Calories: 370 | Protein: 11.2g | Carbs: 46.3g | Fat: 13.2g | Fiber: 7.9g

Ingredients:

- Fifty grams of Brazil nuts
- Three bananas (sliced)
- Three-hundred grams of raspberries
- Maple syrup (for serving)

For batter:

- Four-hundred grams of firm tofu
- Two tsps. of each
    - Lemon juice
    - Vanilla extract
- Four-hundred ml of almond milk
- One tbsp. of vegetable oil
- Two cups of buckwheat flour
- Four tbsps. of sugar
- Two tsps. of mixed spice (ground)
- One tbsp. of baking powder

Method:

1. Preheat your oven at 160 degrees Celsius. Cook the nuts by scattering them in a tray for five minutes. Chop the nuts.

2. Add vanilla, tofu, almond milk, and lemon juice in a deep bowl; blend the mixture using a stick blender. Add oil to the mixture and blend again.

3. Take a large bowl and combine the dry ingredients; add one tsp. of salt and combine. Add the mixture of tofu and combine.

4. Heat a pan and add one tsp. oil in it. Make sure that the pan is not excessively hot.

5. Use a large spoon for dropping three spoons of batter in the pan. Swirl the pan for making the pancake even—Cook for two minutes on each side. Repeat the same for the remaining batter.

6. Serve with berries, bananas, nuts, and drizzle some maple syrup from the top.

Chapter 2: Side Dish Recipes

Side dish plays a profound role in any proper meal. I have included some tasty and easy vegan side dish recipes in this section.

Baked Beans
Total Prep & Cooking Time: Five hours and twenty minutes

Yields: Ten servings

Nutrition Facts: Calories: 249 | Protein: 11.2g | Carbs: 45.3g | Fat: 2.9g | Fiber: 13.7g

Ingredients:

- Sixteen ounces of navy beans (dry)
- Six cups of water
- Two tbsps. of olive oil
- Two cups of sweet onion (chopped)
- One garlic clove (minced)
- Four cans of tomato sauce
- One-fourth cup of brown sugar
- Half cup of molasses
- Three tbsps. of cider vinegar
- Three bay leaves
- One tsp. of mustard (dry)
- One-fourth tsp. of each
  - Black pepper (ground)
  - Nutmeg (ground)
  - Cinnamon (ground)

Method:

1. Add water and beans in a pot and boil the mixture. Lower the flame and cook for one hour. Cook until the beans are tender. Drain the beans and keep aside.

2. Preheat your oven to 160 degrees Celsius.

3. Take an iron skillet and heat oil in it. Add onions in the oil. Cook for two minutes. Add garlic to the pan.

4. Combine the onion mixture with the cooked beans. Add tomato sauce, molasses, vinegar, brown sugar, pepper, bay leaves, cinnamon, mustard, and nutmeg. Mix well.

5. Cover the dish and bake for three hours. Stir in between.

6. Remove the cover and bake for forty minutes.

Baked Potato Wedges

Total Prep & Cooking Time: Fifty-five minutes

Yields: Four servings

Nutrition Facts: Calories: 234 | Protein: 5.1g | Carbs: 42.6g | Fat: 4.3g | Fiber: 8.9g

Ingredients:

- One tbsp. of olive oil
- Eight sweet potatoes (sliced into quarters)
- Half tsp. of paprika

Method:

1. Preheat your oven at 160/180 degrees Celsius.
2. Grease a baking sheet with cooking spray.
3. Combine potatoes and paprika in a bowl. Add the potatoes to the baking sheet.
4. Bake for forty minutes.
5. Serve warm.

Black Beans And Quinoa

Total Prep & Cooking Time: Fifty minutes

Yields: Ten servings

Nutrition Facts: Calories: 143 | Protein: 8.7g | Carbs: 25.6g | Fat: 1.2g | Fiber: 8.7g

Ingredients:

- One tsp. of vegetable oil
- One large onion (chopped)
- Three garlic cloves (chopped)
- Three-fourth cup of quinoa
- Two cups of vegetable stock
- One tsp. of cumin (ground)
- One-fourth tsp. of cayenne powder
- One cup of corn kernels (frozen)
- Two cans of black beans (rinsed)
- Half cup of cilantro (chopped)
- Pepper and salt (according to taste)

Method:

1. Take a medium pan and heat oil in it. Add garlic and onion to the pan. Cook for ten minutes until browned.

2. Add quinoa to the pan and mix well. Cover the mixture with vegetable stock. Season with salt, pepper, and cayenne. Boil the mixture. Cover the pan and simmer for twenty minutes until quinoa gets tender.

3. Add the corn kernels to the pan and simmer for five minutes.

4. Add cilantro and black beans to the mixture.

5. Serve hot.

Roasted Lemon Garlic Broccoli

Total Prep & Cooking Time: Twenty-five minutes

Yields: Six servings

Nutrition Facts: Calories: 48.3 | Protein: 3g | Carbs: 6.9g | Fat: 1.8g | Fiber: 3g

Ingredients:

- Two heads of broccoli (separate the florets)
- Two tsps. of olive oil (extra virgin)
- One tsp. of salt
- Half tsp. of black pepper (ground)
- One garlic clove (minced)
- One-fourth tsp. of lemon juice

Method:

1. Preheat your oven at 180/200 degrees Celsius.
2. Toss the florets of broccoli with olive oil in a bowl. Add pepper, garlic, and salt. Spread the coated broccoli florets on a baking sheet.
3. Bake for twenty minutes.
4. Add lemon juice from the top and serve warm.

Spicy Tofu
Total Prep & Cooking Time: Twenty minutes

Yields: Four servings

Nutrition Facts: Calories: 305.2 | Protein: 20.1g | Carbs: 15.4g | Fat: 19.3g | Fiber: 5.2g

Ingredients:

- Three tbsps. of peanut oil
- One red onion (sliced)
- One pound of tofu (firm, cubed)
- One bell pepper (sliced)
- One chili pepper (chopped)
- Three garlic cloves (crushed)
- One-third cup of hot water
- Two tbsps. of each
    - Soy sauce
    - White vinegar
- One tsp. of cornstarch
- One tbsp. of each
    - Red pepper flakes (crushed)
    - Brown sugar

Method:

1. Take a wok and heat oil in it. Add the tofu to the oil and keep cooking until browned. Add bell pepper, onion, garlic, and chili pepper. Mix well and cook for five minutes.

2. Whisk vinegar, soy sauce, red pepper flakes, brown sugar, and cornstarch in a bowl.

3. Add the mixture of vinegar to the wok and toss well for coating. Simmer the mixture for five minutes.

4. Serve hot.

Spanish Rice

Total Prep & Cooking Time: Forty minutes

Yields: Four servings

Nutrition Facts: Calories: 267.2 | Protein: 4.7g | Carbs: 42.7g | Fat: 5.6g | Fiber: 3g

Ingredients:

- Two tbsps. of vegetable oil
- One cup of white rice (uncooked)
- One onion (chopped)
- Half bell pepper (chopped)
- Two cups of water
- One can of green chilies and diced tomatoes
- Two tsps. of chili powder
- One tsp. of salt

Method:

1. Take a deep skillet and heat oil in it. Add onion, rice, and bell pepper to the skillet. Sauté until onions are soft and rice gets browned.
2. Add tomatoes and water to the skillet. Add salt and chili powder.
3. Simmer the mixture for thirty minutes and cover the skillet.
4. Serve hot.

Pepper And Lemon Pasta

Total Prep & Cooking Time: Twenty minutes

Yields: Eight servings

Nutrition Facts: Calories: 232.8 | Protein: 8.5g | Carbs: 41g | Fat: 4.6g | Fiber: 3.6g

Ingredients:

- One pound of spaghetti
- Two tbsps. of olive oil
- One tbsp. of basil (dried)
  Three tbsps. of lemon juice
- Black pepper (ground, according to taste)

Method:

1. Take a large pot and boil water in it with light salt. Add the pasta to the pot and cook for ten minutes. Drain the pasta.

2. Combine lemon juice, black pepper, lemon juice, and basil in a bowl.

3. Add the lemon mixture to the cooked pasta and toss it properly.

4. Serve cold or hot.

Chapter 3: High Protein Recipes

The vegan diet is rich in proteins, as it is mainly composed of plant compounds. Here are some easy to make vegan high protein recipes for you.

Kale Salad With Spicy Tempeh Bits And Chickpeas

Total Prep & Cooking Time: Forty-five minutes

Yields: Four servings

Nutrition Facts: Calories: 473 | Protein: 25g | Carbs: 41g | Fat: 27.1g | Fiber: 17.3g

Ingredients:

- Eight ounces of tempeh
- One-fourth cup of vegetable oil
- One-fourth tsp. of salt
- Two tsps. of each
    - Garlic powder
    - Onion powder
    - Sweet paprika
- One tsp. of each
    - Lemon pepper
    - Chili powder
- One-eighth tsp. of cayenne powder

For salad:

- 400 grams of kale (chopped)
- One cup of carrots (shredded)
- One can of chickpeas
- Two tbsps. of sesame seeds

For dressing:

- Half cup of rice vinegar

- One-fourth cup of soy sauce
- Two tbsps. of sesame oil
- One tbsp. of ginger (grated)

Method:

1. Boil water with salt in a large pot. Blanch the kale for thirty seconds. Wash blanched kale under running water. Squeeze out excess water from kale and keep aside.

2. Preheat your oven to 180 degrees Celsius.

3. Mix all the spices for tempeh in a mixing bowl.

4. Cut tempeh into very thin slices.

5. Dip each tempeh slice in oil and arrange them on a baking sheet. Line the tray using parchment paper. Sprinkle the mix of spices from the top. Coat well.

6. Bake tempeh for twenty minutes until crispy and brown in color.

7. Take a large bowl and combine the listed ingredients for the salad.

8. Combine the ingredients of dressing in a jar and shake well.

9. Pour the dressing over the prepared salad. Toss well. Make sure the salad gets coated properly with the dressing.

10. Crumble the slices of tempeh over the salad.

Protein Bars

Total Prep & Cooking Time: One hour and twenty minutes

Yields: Ten servings

Nutrition Facts: Calories: 292 | Protein: 13g | Carbs: 37.9g | Fat: 9.6g | Fiber: 2.3g

Ingredients:

For crust:

- Two cups of oat flour
- Six apricots (dried)
- One-fourth cup of each
    - Brown rice syrup
    - Cocoa powder

For layer:

- One cup of oat flour
- Half cup of each
    - Vegan protein powder (chocolate)
    - Rolled oats
- One-fourth tsp. of salt
- Two tbsps. of each
    - Hemp seeds (hulled)
    - Chia seeds
- Half cup of almond butter

- One-fourth cup of any vegan sweetener
- One cup of coconut milk
- One tbsp. flax seeds (ground)

Method:

1. Combine all the ingredients for the crust in a blender. Keep the dough aside.

2. Take a large bowl and mix the dry ingredients for the next layer. You can use a fork for proper mixing.

3. Mix water and flax in a bowl and keep aside until it turns into a gel.

4. Add almond butter, sweetener, coconut milk, and flax gel to the mixture of dry ingredients. Use a fork for mixing properly.

5. Pour the mixture in a food processor and blend well for making it smooth.

6. Use parchment paper for lining a baking sheet. Add the crust to the sheet and press the crust out. Add the next layer on the crust and evenly spread it out.

7. Put the baking sheet in the freezer for one hour.

8. Serve by cutting bars of your desired size and shape.

Tofu And Spinach Scramble

Total Prep & Cooking Time: Thirty minutes

Yields: Two servings

Nutrition Facts: Calories: 319 | Protein: 22.1g | Carbs: 11.4g | Fat: 22g | Fiber: 6.5g

Ingredients:

- Fourteen ounces of tofu (firm, cut into cubes of half-inch)
- Half tsp. of turmeric (ground)
- Black pepper and kosher salt (to taste)
- One-eighth tsp. of cayenne powder (ground)
- Two tbsps. of olive oil (extra virgin)
- Three scallions (sliced)
- Five ounces of spinach (chopped)
- Two tsps. of lemon juice
- One cup of grape tomatoes (halved)
- Half cup of basil (chopped)

Method:

1. Mix turmeric, tofu, one-fourth tsp. of salt, cayenne, and half tsp. of black pepper in a bowl. Toss the ingredients for mixing properly.

2. Take a large skillet and heat oil in it; add the scallions and stir for about one minute. Add tofu mixture and cook for five minutes until the tofu gets browned.

3. Add lemon juice, spinach, and half tsp. of salt to the tofu. Cook for one minute until the spinach wilts. Add tomatoes and stir for one minute.

4. Remove the skillet from heat and add basil.

5. Serve hot.

Vegan Tacos

Total Prep & Cooking Time: Twenty minutes

Yields: Six servings

Nutrition Facts: Calories: 402 | Protein: 29g | Carbs: 71.2g | Fat: 5.4g | Fiber: 20.3g

Ingredients:

- One tsp. of vegetable oil
- Half onion (diced)
- Two tsps. of jalapeno (chopped)

- Twelve ounces of soy chorizo (remove the casing)
- Sixteen ounces of refried black beans
- Twelve tortillas (corn)
- Cilantro (chopped)

Method:

1. Take a skillet and heat oil in it. Add onion and jalapeno to the skillet—Cook for ten minutes. Add chorizo and cook for five minutes.

2. Take a small pan and cook the beans on low heat.

3. Arrange two tortillas for making six tacos in total.

4. Spread the beans on the tortillas; top the beans with the mixture of chorizo. Serve with cilantro from the top.

Grilled Tofu Steaks And Spinach Salad

Total Prep & Cooking Time: One hour

Yields: Two servings

Nutrition Facts: Calories: 154 | Protein: 22g | Carbs: 8g | Fat: 11.3g | Fiber: 9.3g

Ingredients:

For tofu steak:

- Half block of tofu (firm)
- One tbsp. of soy sauce
- One tsp. of each
    - Miso paste

- - Tomato paste
  - Olive oil
- Half tsp. of maple syrup
- One-fourth cup of breadcrumbs

For spinach salad:

- Two cups of baby spinach
- One tbsp. of each
  - Olive oil (extra virgin)
  - Pine nuts
  - Lemon juice
- Pinch of salt
- Pinch of black pepper (ground)

Method:

1. Cut the tofu block in half and squeeze out any excess water. Make sure you do not break the block of tofu. Use paper towels for drying the tofu.

2. Cut the tofu in size and shape of your choice.

3. Take a small mixing bowl and combine tomato paste, soy sauce, olive oil, sesame, miso paste, and maple syrup. Mix until the sauce is smooth.

4. Spread breadcrumbs in a shallow dish.

5. Dip the pieces of tofu in the prepared sauce and then coat them in breadcrumbs. Repeat for the remaining tofu.

6. Grease a grill pan with some olive oil. Add the tofu steaks and cook for fifteen minutes on each side. Cook until both sides are browned.

7. For the salad, mix the listed ingredients in a medium-sized mixing bowl. Toss the ingredients properly.

8. Serve the tofu steaks with spinach salad by the side.

Corn, Quinoa, And Edamame Salad

Total Prep & Cooking Time: Two hours and ten minutes

Yields: Four servings

Nutrition Facts: Calories: 130 | Protein: 18g | Carbs: 13g | Fat: 5.8g | Fiber: 3.1g

Ingredients:

- One cup of corn kernels (frozen)
- Two cups of shelled edamame
- Half cup of cooked quinoa
- One green onion (sliced)
- Half sweet bell pepper (diced)
- Two tbsps. of cilantro (chopped)
- One and a half tbsps. of olive oil
- One tbsp. of each
  - Lime juice
  - Lemon juice
- One-fourth tsp. of each
  - Salt
  - Thyme (dried)
  - Chili powder
  - Black pepper (ground)

Method:

1. Boil corn and edamame in water with a little bit of salt. Drain and keep aside.

2. Take a bowl and mix corn, edamame, quinoa, bell pepper, green onion, and cilantro.

3. Whisk together lemon juice, olive oil, lime juice, chili powder, salt, thyme, and black pepper in a small bowl.

4. Pour the dressing all over the salad. Mix well.

5. Chill in the refrigerator for two hours.

Lentil Soup

Total Prep & Cooking Time: Fifty-five minutes

Yields: Six servings

Nutrition Facts: Calories: 230 | Protein: 9.2g | Carbs: 31.2g | Fat: 8.6g | Fiber: 11.3g

Ingredients:

- Two tbsps. of olive oil (extra virgin)
- One onion (diced)

- Two carrots (diced)
- Two stalks of celery (diced)
- One bell pepper (diced)
- Three garlic cloves (minced)
- One tbsp. of cumin
- One-fourth tsp. of paprika
- One tsp. of oregano
- Two cups of tomatoes (diced)
- Two cans of green lentils (rinsed)
- Eight cups of vegetable stock
- Half tsp. of salt
- Cilantro (for garnishing)
- One ripe avocado (diced)

Method:

1. Heat some oil in a pot. Start adding bell pepper, onion, carrots, and celery to the pot. Sauté the veggies for five minutes until tender; add paprika, cumin, garlic, and oregano. Mix well.

2. Add chilies, tomatoes, stock, salt, and lentils; simmer the mixture for forty minutes. Add pepper and salt according to taste.

3. Serve with avocado and cilantro from the top.

Chapter 4: Dessert Recipes

Everyone loves to have some dessert after having their meals. Desserts can be vegan too. So in this section, I have included some tasty dessert recipes that you can make easily.

Chocolate Pudding

Total Prep & Cooking Time: Forty-five minutes

Yields: Two servings

Nutrition Facts: Calories: 265.1 | Protein: 8.3g | Carbs: 52.2g | Fat: 4.6g | Fiber:

4.9g

Ingredients:

- Three tbsps. of cornstarch
- Two tbsps. of water
- Two cups of soy milk
- One-fourth tsp. of vanilla extract
- One-fourth cup of white sugar
- One cup of cocoa powder

Method:

1. Take a small bowl and mix water and cornstarch for forming a fine paste.

2. Take a saucepan and heat it over medium flame. Add soy milk, sugar, vanilla, a mixture of cornstarch, and cocoa. Stir the mixture until it starts boiling. Keep cooking until the mixture gets thick.

3. Allow the pudding to cool for five minutes.

4. Chill in the fridge for twenty minutes.

Orange Cake

Total Prep & Cooking Time: Forty-five minutes

Yields: Sixteen servings

Nutrition Facts: Calories: 147.3 | Protein: 1.9g | Carbs: 21.6g | Fat: 6.3g | Fiber: 0.8g

Ingredients:

- One large-sized onion (peeled)
- Two cups of flour
- One cup of white sugar
- Half cup of vegetable oil
- One and a half tsps. of baking soda
- Half tsp. of salt

Method:

1. Preheat your oven to 190 degrees Celsius. Grease a baking pan with some oil.
2. Blend the orange in a food processor until it gets completely liquefied.
3. Combine orange juice, sugar, flour, vegetable oil, baking soda, and salt. Pour the cake batter into prepared baking pan.
4. Bake the cake for thirty minutes.

Notes:

- In case you do not want to make orange juice at home, you can use orange juice from the store.
- This cake can be converted into a plain cake by omitting orange juice and using soy milk along with rice milk.

Pumpkin Tofu Pie

Total Prep & Cooking Time: Two hours

Yields: Eight servings

Nutrition Facts: Calories: 229.3 | Protein: 4.7g | Carbs: 33.6g | Fat: 8.6g | Fiber: 3.7g

Ingredients

- Ten ounces of silken tofu (drained)
- One can of pumpkin puree
- Three-fourth cup of white sugar
- Half tsp. of salt
- One tsp. of cinnamon (ground)
- One-fourth tsp. of ginger (ground)
- One-eighth tsp. of cloves (ground)
- One pie crust (unbaked)

Method:

1. Preheat the oven at 220/230 degrees Celsius.
2. Add pumpkin puree, tofu, cinnamon, salt, sugar, clove, and ginger in a food processor. Blend the ingredients until smooth.
3. Pour over the blended mixture into the crust.
4. Bake the pie for fifteen minutes and then reduce the temperature to 175 degrees Celsius. Bake again for forty minutes.
5. Let the pie cool down.
6. Serve at room temperature.

Note: If you are allergic to certain ingredients, check the ingredients of the pie crust.

Vegan Brownie

Total Prep & Cooking Time: Fifty minutes

Yields: Sixteen servings

Nutrition Facts: Calories: 254.3 | Protein: 2.6g | Carbs: 38.3g | Fat: 13.6g | Fiber: 2.8g

Ingredients:

- Two cups of flour
- Two cups of white sugar
- Three-fourth cup of cocoa powder (unsweetened)
- One tsp. of baking powder
- Half tsp. of salt
- One cup of each
    - Vegetable oil
    - Water
- One and a half tsps. of vanilla extract

Method:

1. Preheat your oven at 160/175 degrees Celsius.
2. Take a large bowl and combine sugar, flour, cocoa powder, salt, and baking powder. Add vegetable oil, vanilla extract, and water to the mixture. Mix well for making a smooth batter.
3. Spread the brownie mix in a baking pan.
4. Bake the brownie for thirty minutes.
5. Allow the brownie to cool for ten minutes.
6. Cut in squares and serve.

Vegan Cupcake

Total Prep & Cooking Time: Twenty-five minutes

Yields: Eighteen servings

Nutrition Facts: Calories: 150.2 | Protein: 1.9g | Carbs: 21.6g | Fat: 6.3g | Fiber: 0.9g

Ingredients:

- One tbsp. of cider vinegar
- Two cups of almond milk
- Two and a half cups of flour
- One cup of white sugar
- Two tsps. of baking powder
- Half tsp. of each
    - Salt
    - Baking soda
    - Coconut oil (warmed)
- One and a half tsps. of vanilla extract

Method:

1. Preheat the oven at 160/175 degrees Celsius. Grease eighteen muffin cups using some oil.

2. Mix cider vinegar and almond milk in a bowl. Allow it to stand for five minutes until the mixture gets curdled.

3. Take a bowl and combine sugar, salt, baking powder, flour, and baking soda.

4. Take another bowl and combine coconut oil, vanilla, and almond milk mixture. Add this mixture to the mixture of dry ingredients.

5. Divide the batter into muffin cups—Bake for twenty minutes.

6. Allow the cupcakes to sit for ten minutes.

7. Serve with the desired frosting from the top.

Vanilla Cake

Total Prep & Cooking Time: Fifty minutes

Yields: Eight servings

Nutrition Facts: Calories: 277.9 | Protein: 3.5g | Carbs: 44.2g | Fat: 9.2g | Fiber: 0.9g

Ingredients:

- One cup of soy milk
- One tbsp. of apple cider vinegar
- One and a half cup of flour
- One cup of white sugar
- One tsp. of each
    - Baking powder
    - Baking soda
- Half tsp. of salt
- One-third cup of canola oil
- One-fourth tsp. of almond extract
- One tbsp. of vanilla extract
- One-fourth cup of water

Method:

1. Preheat your oven at about 160/175 degrees Celsius. Grease a baking pan with some oil.

2. Mix vinegar and soy milk in a large cup.

3. Combine sugar, flour, salt, baking soda, and baking powder in a bowl.

4. Add lemon juice, canola oil, vanilla extract, almond extract, and water to the mixture of soy milk. Stir the mixture of soy milk into the mixture of flour. Mix well until there is no lump.

5. Pour the cake batter in the baking dish.

6. Bake in the preheated oven for thirty-five minutes.

Miracle Fudge

Total Prep & Cooking Time: One hour and ten minutes

Yields: Twenty-four servings

Nutrition Facts: Calories: 77.3 | Protein: 0.9g | Carbs: 4.9g | Fat: 6.2g | Fiber: 1.2g

Ingredients:

- Half cup of cocoa (unsweetened)
- One cup of maple syrup
- One tsp. of vanilla extract
- One pinch of salt
- One-third cup of each
    - Chopped walnuts
    - Coconut oil (melted)
- One tsp. of cocoa powder (unsweetened, for dusting)

Method:

1. Add half cup of cocoa powder in a bowl along with maple syrup; give it a stir. Add vanilla extract and salt. Add melted coconut oil and combine well.

2. Add walnuts in a pan and toast them for one minute.

3. Add the toasted walnuts to the fudge. Mix well.

4. Pour the mixture of fudge into a silicone mold. Smoothen the top.

5. Wrap the silicone mold using plastic wrap and put it in the freezer for thirty minutes. Take out the fudge pieces from the mold and dust with cocoa powder from the top.

6. Serve cold.

Chapter 5: Sauces & Dips Recipes

Sauces and dips are important components of any meal that can make the food tastier. Here are some vegan sauces and dips recipes for you.

Tomato Jam
Total Prep & Cooking Time: Forty-five minutes

Yields: One full cup

Nutrition Facts: Calories: 34 | Protein: 0.2g | Carbs: 8.6g | Fat: 0.1g | Fiber: 0.2g

Ingredients:

- Two pounds of plum tomatoes
- One-fourth cup of coconut sugar
- Half tsp. of salt
- One-fourth tsp. of paprika
- One tsp. of vinegar (white wine)
- Black pepper (to taste)

Method:

1. Take a large pot and boil water in it; add the tomatoes to the water and boil for one minute. Remove the tomatoes and put them in an ice-water bath.

2. Peel the blanched tomatoes and chop them.

3. Add chopped tomatoes in a pot over a medium flame. Add sugar and stir the mixture—Cook for ten minutes.

4. Add pepper, salt, and paprika. Simmer for ten minutes until the jam thickens.

5. Remove from heat and add white wine vinegar. Serve with crackers, burgers, toasts, etc.

Walnut Kale Pesto

Total Prep & Cooking Time: Thirty minutes

Yields: One small bowl

Nutrition Facts: Calories: 240 | Protein: 3.6g | Carbs: 2.6g | Fat: 22.3g | Fiber: 0.8g

Ingredients:

- Half bunch of kale (chopped)
- Half cup of walnuts (chopped)
- Two garlic cloves (minced)
- One-fourth cup of yeast
- One cup of olive oil
- Three tbsps. of lemon juice
- Pepper and salt (for seasoning)

Method:

1. Take a pot and boil water in it. Add kale to the pot with one tsp. of salt—Cook for five minutes.
2. Add kale, garlic, walnuts, olive oil, yeast, along with lemon juice in a food processor. Add pepper and salt according to your taste. Blend well.

Ranch Dressing

Total Prep & Cooking Time: Thirty minutes

Yields: One small bowl

Nutrition Facts: Calories: 92 | Protein: 0.1g | Carbs: 1g | Fat: 9.1g | Fiber: 0.4g

Ingredients:

- One cup of vegan mayo
- Half tsp. of each
    - Onion powder
    - Garlic powder
- One-fourth tsp. of black pepper (ground)
- Two tsps. of parsley (chopped)
- One tbsp. of dill (chopped)
- Half cup of soy milk (unsweetened)

Method:

1. Mix the listed ingredients in a medium mixing bowl.
2. If you want the dressing to be thin, add a bit of almond milk. Allow the dressing to sit for a few minutes.
3. Chill the prepared dressing.

Notes:

- You can serve the dressing with any savory snacks, sandwiches, quick-bites, salads, etc.
- You can store the leftover dressing in the fridge for two days.
- You can add some ground nuts for enhancing the flavor

PART II

Vegan Keto

The ketogenic diet is a popular diet that is low in carbohydrates and is high in fat. The diet involves moderate consumption of protein that can promote weight loss and can also help in the improvement of overall health. Although the keto diet is mostly associated with animal-based foods, it can also be adapted for fitting food items that are plant-based, specifically vegan diets. The vegan diet does not include any kind of animal product. But, with proper planning, even vegans can enjoy the benefits of the keto diet.

In keto diet, carbs are reduced to 45-50 grams per day for maintaining and reaching ketosis. Ketosis is a metabolic process of the body for burning fat as fuel in place of glucose. People who follow a vegan keto diet rely on plant-based foods such as grains, veggies, and fruits. As the requirement of fat is more, plant-based food products such as avocados, coconut oil, nuts, and seeds are included in the vegan keto diet. Vegan keto diet comes along with various benefits. It can reduce the overall risk of developing severe health conditions like diabetes, heart diseases, and specific cancers. For instance, studies revealed that all those who follow vegan keto diet have a 74% lower risk of high blood pressure and a 75% risk reduction for type 2 diabetes.

It has also been found that people who follow a vegan keto diet can lose more weight than those who eat animal-based food products. The vegan keto diet can also increase the level of adiponectin, a protein responsible for regulating blood sugar and fat metabolism. When the level of adiponectin is high, it can help in the reduction of inflammation, better control over blood sugar, and can also help in reducing diseases related to obesity. Keto diet has also shown evident results in reducing the risk factors of heart diseases, along with LDL cholesterol, blood pressure, and high triglycerides. Combining a vegan diet along with a ketogenic diet can effectively impact your overall health.

When you start following a vegan diet, you will need to reduce the intake of carbs and replace them with healthy fats. You will also need to include vegan high protein sources. You cannot consume animal-based products such as poultry, egg, meat, seafood, and dairy. Here are some examples of the food items that you will need to avoid altogether:

- **Dairy:** Butter, milk, yogurt
- **Poultry and meat:** Turkey, pork, beef, chicken
- **Egg:** Egg yolk and egg white
- **Animal-based items:** Whey protein, egg white protein, honey
- **Seafood:** Shrimp, fish, mussels, clams

Here are some examples of the food items that you will need to reduce:

- **Sugar-based drinks:** Soda, juice, sweet tea, sports drinks, smoothies
- **Starches and grains:** Bread, cereal, pasta, baked items
- **Starchy veggies:** Sweet potatoes, potatoes, beet, squash, peas

Turn to the next page for recipes that can help you get started with a vegan keto diet.

Chapter 1: Breakfast Recipes

Breakfast is an important part of any diet plan. Here are some tasty vegan keto recipes for you.

Tofu Scramble

Total Prep & Cooking Time: Twenty minutes

Yields: Two servings

Nutrition Facts: Calories: 204 | Protein: 21.3g | Carbs: 3.6g | Fat: 12.3g | Fiber: 0.8g

Ingredients:

- Two-hundred grams of tofu (firm)
- One tbsp. of vegan butter
- Two tbsps. of nutritional yeast
- Half tsp. of each
    - Paprika
    - Turmeric
    - Garlic powder
- One tsp. of Dijon mustard
- One-fourth tsp. of each
    - Onion powder
    - Black salt
- One-third cup of soy milk

Method:

1. Place tofu in a bowl. Use a fork for mashing the tofu. Leave some medium-sized chunks.

2. Add turmeric, yeast, paprika, garlic powder, Dijon mustard, onion powder, and black salt in a bowl. Combine the ingredients. Add soy milk and whisk properly for making a smooth sauce.

3. Add vegan butter to a medium pan. Add mashed tofu and fry it for two minutes until browned. Add prepared sauce to the mashed tofu. Combine well. Cook for five minutes until the sauce gets absorbed by the tofu.

4. Serve hot.

Low Carb Pancakes

Total Prep & Cooking Time: Thirty minutes

Yields: Two servings

Nutrition Facts: Calories: 249 | Protein: 10.4g | Carbs: 12.8g | Fat: 19.6g | Fiber: 9.8g

Ingredients:

- Two tbsps. of almond butter
- One-fourth cup of almond milk (unsweetened)

- One tbsp. of coconut flour
- One and a half tbsps. of ground flax
- Half tsp. of baking powder

Method:

1. Take a small bowl and combine the almond milk with almond butter.

2. Take another bowl and combine the dry ingredients.

3. Add the mixture of milk to the dry mixture. Combine well. Allow the batter to sit for five minutes.

4. Heat a skillet over medium flame.

5. Add one spoon of batter to the warm skillet. Evenly spread out the batter—Cook the pancakes for five minutes on each side. Repeat the same for the remaining batter.

6. Serve the pancakes hot with almond butter from the top.

Cauliflower Hashbrowns

Total Prep & Cooking Time: Fifty minutes

Yields: Six servings

Nutrition Facts: Calories: 142 | Protein: 6.3g | Carbs: 18.2g | Fat: 5.6g | Fiber: 4.3g

Ingredients:

- Half head of cauliflower (separate the florets)
- One tbsp. of coconut oil
- Half onion (chopped)
- One-fourth cup of chickpea flour
- One tbsp. of cornstarch
- Half tsp. of each
    - Salt
    - Garlic powder
- Two tbsps. of water

Method:

1. Preheat your oven at 200 degrees Celsius; use parchment paper for lining a baking sheet. Spray the parchment paper with some oil.
2. Add onion and cauliflower in a blender and blend until crumbly.
3. Combine chickpea flour, cornstarch, salt, garlic powder, and water in a bowl. Mix well.
4. Add the cauliflower crumbles to the batter. Combine properly.
5. Shape the hashbrowns into thick patties.
6. Bake the hashbrowns in the oven for forty minutes. Flip the patties halfway.
7. Serve hot.

Vanilla Waffles

Total Prep & Cooking Time: Twenty minutes

Yields: Two servings

Nutrition Facts: Calories: 160 | Protein: 21.3g | Carbs: 13.6g | Fat: 4.9g | Fiber: 9.9g

Ingredients:

- One-fourth cup of oat flour
- Half scoop of protein powder (vanilla)
- One tbsp. of each
    - Flaxseed (ground)
    - Granulated sweetener of your choice
- One-fourth tsp. of baking powder
- Half cup of almond milk
- One-fourth tsp. of vanilla extract

Method:

1. Add the dry ingredients in a large bowl. Combine well.
2. Add baking powder, flaxseed, vanilla extract, and one-fourth cup of the almond milk in a bowl. Whisk well and allow it to sit for four minutes.
3. Add the dry ingredients to the mixture of vanilla extract. Combine properly.
4. Heat up a waffle iron and add two spoons of waffle mixture.
5. Cook for four minutes.
6. Serve hot.

Pecan And Cinnamon Porridge

Total Prep & Cooking Time: Twenty minutes

Yields: Two servings

Nutrition Facts: Calories: 580 | Protein: 13.4g | Carbs: 5.1g | Fat: 49.7g | Fiber: 10.8g

Ingredients:

- One-fourth cup of coconut milk
- One cup of almond butter
- Three-fourth cup of almond milk
- One tbsp. of coconut oil
- Two tbsps. of chia seeds
- Three tbsps. of hemp seeds
- One-fourth cup of each
    - Pecans
    - Flaked coconut
- Half tsp. of cinnamon

Method:

1. Mix almond milk, coconut milk, coconut oil, and almond butter in a pan. Simmer the mixture over a medium flame.

2. Once the mixture gets hot, remove from heat.

3. Add hemp seeds, chia seeds, pecans, and coconut flakes. Combine the ingredients and add cinnamon. Allow the porridge to sit for ten minutes.

4. Serve cold or hot with coconut flakes from the top.

Chapter 2: Appetizers Recipes

Appetizers play an important role in a complete meal. There are various vegan keto appetizers that you can include in your diet plan. Let's have a look at them.

Arugula Salad

Total Prep & Cooking Time: Ten minutes

Yields: Two servings

Nutrition Facts: Calories: 41 | Protein: 0.7g | Carbs: 2.6g | Fat: 3.1g | Fiber: 0.9g

Ingredients:

- Six tbsps. of olive oil (extra virgin)
- Two tbsps. of lemon juice
- Salt and pepper (according to taste)
- Four cups of arugula

Method:

1. Take a small-sized bowl and whisk together olive oil and lemon juice. Add pepper and salt.

2. Add the arugula in a large bowl and add the dressing from the top. Toss to combine.

Cauliflower Soup

Total Prep & Cooking Time: Thirty minutes

Yields: Four servings

Nutrition Facts: Calories: 127 | Protein: 5.2g | Carbs: 15.6g | Fat: 5.6g | Fiber: 3.9g

Ingredients:

- One tbsp. of olive oil (extra virgin)
- One yellow onion (chopped)

- One garlic clove (minced)
- One cauliflower (florets separated)
- Six cups of vegetable stock
- Three sprigs of thyme
- One bay leaf
- Pepper and salt (to taste)
- One-fourth cup of vegan cream

Method:

1. Take a deep pot and heat oil in it. Add onions and cook it for six minutes until tender. Add minced garlic to the pot. Add the florets of cauliflower, thyme, vegetable stock, and bay leaf. Simmer the mixture for twenty minutes until the florets are tender.

2. Remove bay leaf along with thyme. Blend the mixture using a stick blender until smooth. Add vegan cream and simmer for five minutes.

3. Serve with olive oil from the top.

Cauliflower Zucchini Fritters

Total Prep & Cooking Time: Twenty minutes

Yields: Eight servings

Nutrition Facts: Calories: 53 | Protein: 4.2g | Carbs: 5.9g | Fat: 2.1g | Fiber: 3.6g

Ingredients:

- Half head of a cauliflower
- Two large zucchinis
- One-fourth cup of flour
- Half tsp. of salt
- One-fourth tsp. of black pepper (ground)

Method:

1. Add zucchini in a blender and grate.
2. Add the cauliflower to the food processor and blend into small chunks.
3. Put the veggies in a dishtowel and squeeze out as much water as possible.
4. Transfer the veggies to a bowl; add flour, pepper, and salt. Mix well.
5. Shape the mixture into small patties.
6. Heat oil in a pan. Add the patties to the pan—Cook for three minutes on all sides.
7. Serve hot with any dipping sauce of your choice.

Notes:

- You can add chickpeas for extra flavor.
- The leftover fritters can be stored in the fridge for two days.

Zucchini Noodles And Avocado Sauce

Total Prep & Cooking Time: Thirty minutes

Yields: Two servings

Nutrition Facts: Calories: 311 | Protein: 6.7g | Carbs: 17.8g | Fat: 24.5g | Fiber: 9.9g

Ingredients:

- One large zucchini
- Two cups of basil
- One-third cup of water
- Four tbsps. of pine nuts
- Two tbsps. of lemon juice
- One large avocado
- Twelve cherry tomatoes (sliced)

Method:

1. Start with the zucchini noodles. Use a peeler or a spiralizer for making the noodles. In case you do not have a peeler or spiralizer, use a sharp knife for cutting thin strips of zucchini.

2. Add all the ingredients in the food processor except for the cherry tomatoes.

3. Combine sauce, noodles, and cherry tomatoes in a bowl. Toss for combining.

4. Serve at room temperature, or you can also chill in the freezer for ten minutes.

Notes:

- You can add any fresh herbs and veggies that you want to. You can replace zucchini with other vegetables such as carrots, cabbage, beet, squash, etc.

- Pine nuts can be replaced with any nuts of your choice.

- You can store the leftover noodles in the fridge for two days.

Roasted Brussels Sprouts

Total Prep & Cooking Time: Thirty minutes

Yields: Four servings

Nutrition Facts: Calories: 130 | Protein: 3.8g | Carbs: 11.3g | Fat: 9.7g | Fiber: 4.6g

Ingredients:

- Four-hundred grams of Brussels sprouts (halved)
- Two tbsps. of olive oil
- Black pepper and salt (according to taste)

Method:

1. Preheat your oven to 220 degrees Celsius.

2. Take a large baking sheet. Spread the Brussels sprouts on the sheet. Drizzle olive oil from the top. Season with pepper and salt. Toss for combining.

3. Roast the sprouts in the oven for twenty-five minutes until all the are crispy outside and tender from inside.

4. Serve hot.

Chapter 3: Main Course Recipes

After you are done with the appetizers, now it is time to have a look at the main course recipes. I have included some tasty vegan keto main course recipes in this section that you can enjoy in your lunch and dinner as well.

Mushroom Tomato Spaghetti Squash

Total Prep & Cooking Time: Forty minutes

Yields: Four servings

Nutrition Facts: Calories: 240 | Protein: 6.3g | Carbs: 21.3g | Fat: 8.9g | Fiber:

8.6g

Ingredients:

- Six cups of spaghetti squash (cooked)
- Two cups of tomatoes (diced)
- Four garlic cloves (minced)
- Eight ounces of mushrooms (sliced)
- One-third cup of onions (chopped)
- One-fourth cup of pine nuts (toasted)
- A handful of basil
- Three tbsps. of olive oil
- Black pepper and salt (for seasoning)

Method:

1. Cook the spaghetti squash in the way you like. The easiest way to cook is by roasting in the oven. When the squash is cool enough, remove the seeds along with the stringy bits. Shred the squash with a fork. Keep aside.

2. Take a sauté pan and heat some oil in it. Add mushrooms and onions to the pan. Keep cooking for four minutes until onion turns translucent. Add minced garlic to the pan and cook for two minutes. Add tomatoes and keep stirring.

3. Add the cooked spaghetti squash to the mixture and toss it well for combining. Add pine nuts and basil—season with salt and black pepper.

4. Serve hot.

Vegan Shakshuka

Total Prep & Cooking Time: Twenty-five minutes

Yields: Two servings

Nutrition Facts: Calories: 274 | Protein: 21.3g | Carbs: 22.6g | Fat: 9.5g | Fiber: 9.7g

Ingredients:

- One tbsp. of olive oil
- Four garlic cloves
- One can of diced tomatoes
- Pepper and salt (according to taste)
- Two tsps. of dried herbs
- Half tsp. of chili flakes (dried)
- One medium-sized block of tofu
- Black salt (optional)

Method:

1. Take a large skillet and add olive in it. Heat the oil and add garlic to the skillet. Brown the garlic a bit.
2. Add diced tomatoes, pepper, salt, chili flakes, and dried herbs. Mix the ingredients properly and simmer for five minutes.
3. Cut the tofu block in rounds and add them to the skillet.
4. Lower the flame and simmer the shakshuka for fifteen minutes. Cook until the sauce thickens, and the tofu rounds are tender.
5. Sprinkle some black salt from the top.
6. Serve with crusty bread slices or toast by the side.

Zucchini Lasagna

Total Prep & Cooking Time: One hour and twenty minutes

Yields: Eight servings

Nutrition Facts: Calories: 392 | Protein: 6.3g | Carbs: 18.7g | Fat: 33.9g | Fiber: 7.6g

Ingredients:

For vegan ricotta:

- Three cups of macadamia nuts (raw)
- Two tbsps. of nutritional yeast
- Half cup of basil (chopped)
- Two tsps. of oregano (dried)

- One medium-sized lemon (juiced)
- One tbsp. of olive oil (extra virgin)
- One tsp. of each
    - Black pepper
    - Salt
- One-third cup of water

Other ingredients:

- One jar of marinara sauce
- Three medium-sized zucchini squash (sliced thinly)

Method:

1. Preheat your oven at 160/175 degrees Celsius.
2. Add the nuts to a blender and blend. Scrape down the sides. Blend for making a fine meal.
3. Add yeast, oregano, basil, olive oil, lemon juice, pepper, water, and salt to the blended nuts in the blender. Blend for making a smooth paste.
4. Adjust the taste by adding seasonings. If you want more cheesiness, add yeast.
5. Pour one cup of marinara sauce in a baking dish. Line the dish with zucchini slices.
6. Add one scoop of ricotta mixture over the zucchini layer and spread evenly. Repeat for the remaining layers.
7. Cover the baking dish using foil and bake the lasagna for forty-five minutes. Remove the foil. Bake again for fifteen minutes.
8. Allow the lasagna to cool down for ten minutes.
9. Serve warm with basil from the top.

Arugula Tomato And Avocado Salad

Total Prep & Cooking Time: Fifteen minutes

Yields: Four servings

Nutrition Facts: Calories: 259 | Protein: 4.2g | Carbs: 5.2g | Fat: 17g | Fiber: 0.9g

Ingredients:

- One cup of cherry tomatoes (halved)
- Half cup of yellow cherry tomatoes (halved)
- Five ounces of arugula (chopped)
- Two large avocados (cut in chunks)
- Half cup of red onion (diced)
- Six leaves of basil (sliced)

For vinaigrette:

- Two tbsps. of balsamic vinegar
- One tbsp. of each:
    - Maple syrup
    - Olive oil
    - Lemon juice
- One clove of garlic (minced)
- Half tsp. of Italian seasoning
- One-fourth tsp. of each:
    - Pepper
    - Sea salt

Method:

1. Combine tomatoes, arugula, basil, red onion, and chunks of avocado in a mixing bowl.

2. Whisk together olive oil, lemon juice, vinegar, maple syrup, garlic, pepper, salt, and Italian seasoning in a small bowl. Mix well.

3. Add the dressing to the salad mix. Toss well for combining.

4. Serve with basil from the top.

Mushroom Fried Rice

Total Prep & Cooking Time: Thirty minutes

Yields: Six servings

Nutrition Facts: Calories: 118 | Protein: 10.2g | Carbs: 14.9g | Fat: 2.8g | Fiber: 7.3g

Ingredients:

- Four tbsps. of water
- One onion (diced)
- Two-inch piece of ginger (grated)
- Three cloves of garlic (minced)
- Ten ounces mix of veggies (carrots, peas, and edamame)
- Two cups of mushrooms (shitake)
- Four cups of cauliflower rice
- Three tbsps. of tamari
- Half tsp. of sesame oil
- One-fourth cup of green onion (sliced)

Method:

1. Take a large pan and add water to it. Sauté the onions in water for four minutes until translucent and soft; add ginger and garlic to the pan. Stir and cook the mixture for three minutes.

2. Add a mixture of veggies to the pan along with the mushrooms. Stir well for combining. Add the cauliflower rice and mix well. Let the fried rice cook for fifteen minutes until the water dissolves.

3. Add half tsp. of sesame oil and three tsps. of tamari. Stir again.

4. Serve hot with green onions from the top.

Note: You can store the leftover fried rice in the fridge for one day.

Chapter 4: Snacks And Dessert Recipes

Everyone loves to have some snacks in between their meals and a good dessert after having a sumptuous meal. So, I have included some tasty and easy snacks and dessert recipes in this section that you can include in your vegan keto diet.

Almond Flour Crackers

Total Prep & Cooking Time: Twenty-five minutes

Yields: Six servings

Nutrition Facts: Calories: 149 | Protein: 4.2g | Carbs: 5.7g | Fat: 12.3g | Fiber: 3.2g

Ingredients:

- One cup of almond flour
- Two tbsps. of sunflower seeds
- One tbsp. of flax meal or psyllium husks
- Three-fourth tsp. of sea salt
- Three tbsps. of water
- One tbsp. of coconut oil

Method:

1. Preheat your oven at 160/175 degrees Celsius.

2. Add sunflower seeds, almond flour, sea salt, and flax meal in a food processor. Process the ingredients.

3. Add the coconut oil along with water to the mixture and pulse again. Blend until a dough forms.

4. Add the dough on parchment paper and flatten the dough using your hands. Cover the cracker dough using another parchment paper and flatten with the help of a rolling pin.

5. Remove the upper layer sheet of parchment paper. Cut the dough into several crackers into the size and shape that you want.

6. Sprinkle some sea salt from the top.

7. Bake the crackers for fifteen minutes at 175 degrees Celsius until the edges are crisp and brown.

Guacamole

Total Prep & Cooking Time: Twenty minutes

Yields: Four servings

Nutrition Facts: Calories: 180.2 | Protein: 2.3g | Carbs: 12.1g | Fat: 15.2g | Fiber: 7.9g

Ingredients:

- Three ripe avocados
- Half onion (diced)
- Two tomatoes (diced)
- Three tbsps. of cilantro (chopped)
- One jalapeno pepper (diced)
- Two cloves of garlic (minced)
- One lime (juiced)
- Half tsp. of sea salt

Method:

1. Slice the avocado and remove the pit. Skin them and place them in a bowl.
2. Use a fork for mashing the avocados. You can either make it smooth or chunky.
3. Add remaining ingredients and mix well.
4. Serve with crackers.

Strawberry And Avocado Ices

Total Prep & Cooking Time: One hour and ten minutes

Yields: Four servings

Nutrition Facts: Calories: 93 | Protein: 3.1g | Carbs: 4.2g | Fat: 7.2g | Fiber: 4g

Ingredients:

- Two-hundred grams of strawberries (chopped)
- One avocado (chopped)
- Two tsps. of balsamic vinegar
- Half tsp. of vanilla extract
- Two tsps. of maple syrup

Method:

1. Add avocado, strawberries, vanilla, and vinegar in a bowl. Use a hand blender for pulsing the mixture. You can also use a food processor. Blend for reaching the consistency that you want. Add maple syrup and mix again.

2. Pour the mixture into small containers and add strawberry slices from the top. Cover the containers using a plastic wrap.

3. Freeze the containers for one hour.

4. Allow the containers to sit at room temperature for five minutes before serving.

Chocolate And Peanut Butter Ice Cream

Total Prep & Cooking Time: Three hours and ten minutes

Yields: Six servings

Nutrition Facts: Calories: 360 | Protein: 5.8g | Carbs: 7.9g | Fat: 34g | Fiber: 4.2g

Ingredients:

- One can of coconut milk
- Half cup of each
    - Powdered sweetener of your choice
    - Peanut butter
- One-third cup of coconut oil
- One-fourth cup of cocoa powder
- One pinch of salt

Method:

1. Add the ingredients in a blender. Keep blending until smooth.

2. Pour the ice cream mixture in a glass container. Cover the container and freeze for half an hour.

3. Remove the cover and stir the mixture, especially from the sides right to the center. Cover again and freeze for thirty minutes. Stir the mixture once again and freeze for two hours.

4. Scoop the ice cream into serving bowls and garnish with peanut butter from the top.

Carrot Cake

Total Prep & Cooking Time: One hour

Yields: Six servings

Nutrition Facts: Calories: 150 | Protein: 3.1g | Carbs: 4.1g | Fat: 6.3g | Fiber: 3.2g

Ingredients:

- Two cups of flour
- One and a half cup of almond flour
- One-fourth tsp. of baking soda
- One tbsp. of cinnamon
- One tsp. of nutmeg
- One carrot (shredded)
- One-third cup of walnuts (chopped)
- Two tbsps. of shredded coconut
- Half tbsp. of apple cider vinegar
- Three-fourth cup of vegan milk (any vegan milk of your choice)
- Half cup of olive oil
- One-fourth cup of maple syrup

Method:

1. Start by preheating your oven at 180 degrees Celsius. Use parchment paper for lining a square baking pan.

2. Combine maple syrup, olive oil, milk of your choice, and vinegar in a bowl. Add walnuts, carrots, and coconut to the mixture. Mix well.

3. Add flour, almond flour, spices, and baking soda. Combine the ingredients.

4. Pour the prepared batter in the lined pan. Bake the mixture for half an hour.

5. Allow the cake to cool down for five minutes.

6. Serve warm with a frosting of your choice.

Notes:

- Before baking the cake, add some shredded carrots from the top for extra flavor. It will make the cake look beautiful, as well.

- In case you have any leftover cake, you can store it in the fridge for one day.

- You can use almond milk for the best results.

Almond And Chocolate Pudding

Total Prep & Cooking Time: Five hours and ten minutes Yields: Three servings

Nutrition Facts: Calories: 280 | Protein: 5.2g | Carbs: 11.7g | Fat: 24.6g | Fiber: 8.9g

Ingredients:

- Two cups of almond milk
- Half cup of coconut cream
- Three tbsps. of vegan sweetener (of your choice)
- One avocado (pitted)
- Three tbsps. of cocoa powder
- One tsp. of vanilla extract
- Two tsps. of almond extract
- Sliced almonds (to garnish)

Method:

1. Add the listed ingredients in a high-power food processor. Blend the ingredients until smooth.
2. Pour the mixture into serving cups. Cover the cups and refrigerate for about five hours.
3. Serve with sliced almonds from the top.

Notes:

- This pudding is gluten-free and is ketogenic as well.
- You can add chocolate chips from the top for extra flavor.
- You can store the leftover pudding in the fridge for two days.

PART III

Vegetarian Cookbook

The vegetarian diet has gained immense popularity in the last few years. According to some studies, it has been found that an estimated 18% of the world population is vegetarian. Apart from all the environmental and ethical benefits of removing meat from the diet, a properly planned vegetarian diet can reduce the risk of various chronic diseases, improve diet quality, and help in losing weight. The vegetarian diet also does not include poultry and fish. The majority of the people opt for a vegetarian diet for personal or religious reasons and for ethical reasons, such as animal rights. Other people opt for it for various environmental reasons, like livestock production, which results in the emission of greenhouse gases.

A vegetarian diet comes along with a wide array of benefits. It has been found that vegetarians have a better quality of diet when compared to meat-eaters. They also have a higher intake of beneficial nutrients, such as vitamin C, fiber, magnesium, and vitamin E. Switching from a normal meat diet to a vegetarian diet can result to be an effective strategy in case you want to lose weight. For instance, in a review of twelve studies, it has been found that vegetarians can lose about four pounds of weight over eighteen weeks than non-vegetarians. Also, vegetarians have lower BMI or body mass index than non-vegetarians.

Some research found that a vegetarian diet can be linked to a lower risk of developing cancer and those of the colon, breast, stomach, and rectum. However, it lacks enough evidence to prove that a vegetarian diet can effectively reduce cancer risk. People who follow a vegetarian diet can maintain healthy levels of blood sugar. It can also help in preventing the onset of diabetes by controlling the levels of blood sugar. Vegetarian diets help in the reduction of various heart diseases that can make your heart stronger and healthier.

A vegetarian diet needs to include a wide mixture of veggies, fruits, healthy fats, grains, and proteins. To replace the protein that you get from meat in a diet, you will need to include plant foods rich in proteins such as seeds, nuts, legumes, seitan, tofu, and tempeh. Consuming whole foods rich in nutrients, such as vegetables and fruits, can provide your body with the necessary minerals and vitamins to fill the nutritional gaps in a diet. Some of the food items that you can include in your diet are:

- **Fruits:** Bananas, apples, melons, oranges, peaches, pears
- **Vegetables:** Asparagus, leafy greens, carrots, broccoli
- **Legumes:** Beans, lentils, chickpeas, peas
- **Seeds:** Chia, flaxseed, hemp
- **Nuts:** Walnuts, cashews, almonds
- **Proteins:** Seitan, natto, tofu, eggs, tempeh

You cannot include food items such as fish, seafood, meat, poultry, and ingredients that are based on meat. Restriction of eggs and dairy products are applicable for the vegans and not for vegetarians. I have included some tasty and easy vegetarian recipes that will help you to plan your diet effectively.

Chapter 1: Breakfast Recipes

No matter which diet you follow, breakfast is very important in all cases. In this section, you will find some easy-to-make and tasty breakfast recipes that you can include in your vegetarian diet.

Black Bean Bowl

Total Prep & Cooking Time: Fifteen minutes

Yields: Two servings

Nutrition Facts: Calories: 620.1 | Protein: 28.9g | Carbs: 47.6g | Fat: 37.1g | Fiber: 23.2g

Ingredients:

- Two tbsps. of olive oil
- Four eggs (beaten)

- One can of black beans (rinsed)
- One avocado (sliced)
- One-fourth cup of salsa
- One tsp. of each
    - Black pepper (ground)
    - Salt

Method:

1. Take a small pan and heat oil in it. Add the eggs and scramble for five minutes.
2. Place the beans in a bowl. Heat the beans in the oven for one minute.
3. Divide the beans into two serving bowls.
4. Top the beans with scrambled eggs, salsa, and avocado. Add pepper and salt according to taste.

Coconut Blueberry Ricotta Bowl

Total Prep & Cooking Time: Twenty minutes

Yields: One serving

Nutrition Facts: Calories: 303.2 | Protein: 9.5g | Carbs: 32.1g | Fat: 15.3g | Fiber: 3.9g

Ingredients:

- One-fourth cup of ricotta cheese
- One tbsp. of each
    - Honey
    - Coconut milk
    - Slivered almonds
    - Coconut flakes
- Half cup of blueberries

Method:

1. Combine coconut milk and ricotta in a medium-sized bowl. Drizzle honey from the top and add coconut and almonds.
2. Serve with blueberries from the top.

Broccoli Quiche

Total Prep & Cooking Time: Fifty minutes

Yields: Six servings

Nutrition Facts: Calories: 378.2 | Protein: 17.3g | Carbs: 21.1g | Fat: 25.8g | Fiber: 3.1g

Ingredients:

- One pie crust (unbaked)
- Three tbsps. of butter
- One onion (minced)
- One tsp. of each
    - Garlic (minced)
    - Salt
- Two cups of broccoli (chopped)
- One and a half cup of mozzarella cheese (shredded)
- Four eggs (beaten)
- Two and a half cup of milk
- Half tsp. of black pepper
- One tbsp. of butter (melted)

Method:

1. Start by preheating your oven at 175 degrees Celsius. Use pie crust for lining a deep pie pan.

2. Take a large saucepan and add butter to it. Add broccoli, onion, and garlic. Cook the veggies slowly until tender. Add the cooked veggies to the pie crust and add cheese from the top.

3. Mix milk and eggs in a bowl; add pepper and salt for seasoning. Add the remaining butter to the milk mixture. Pour the mixture over the mixture of vegetables.

4. Bake the quiche in the oven for forty minutes or until the center has properly set.

Tomato Bagel Sandwich

Total Prep & Cooking Time: Twenty minutes

Yields: One serving

Nutrition Facts: Calories: 346.3 | Protein: 13.1g | Carbs: 48.6g | Fat: 10.7g | Fiber: 2.9g

Ingredients:

- One bagel (split, toasted)
- Two tbsps. of cream cheese
- One large tomato (sliced thinly)
- Pepper and salt (to season)
- Four basil leaves

Method:

1. Spread the cream cheese on the halves of the bagel.
2. Top the cheese layer with slices of tomato. Add pepper and salt for seasoning.
3. Serve with basil leaves from the top.

Cornmeal And Blueberry Pancakes

Total Prep & Cooking Time: Thirty minutes

Yields: Six servings

Nutrition Facts: Calories: 180.3 | Protein: 5.2g | Carbs: 26.8g | Fat: 5.1g | Fiber: 4.6g

Ingredients:

- One cup of soy milk
- Half cup of each
    - Water
    - Cornmeal (ground)
- One and a half cup of wheat flour
- One tsp. baking powder
- One-third tsp. baking soda
- One-fourth tsp. of salt
- One cup of blueberries
- Two tbsps. of vegetable oil

Method:

1. Preheat your oven at 95 degrees Celsius.

2. Combine water and soy milk in a bowl.

3. Take a large mixing bowl and combine cornmeal, baking soda, flour, salt, and baking powder. Add the mixture of soy milk. Combine properly. Add the blueberries and allow the batter to rest for five minutes.

4. Take a large skillet and grease it using oil. Add one-fourth cup of the batter in the skillet. Cook until the pancakes are bubbly on the top, and the edges are dry. Cook for five minutes on each side. Repeat with the remaining batter.

5. Serve hot with jam or syrup.

Breakfast Tortilla

Total Prep & Cooking Time: Twenty minutes

Yields: Two servings

Nutrition Facts: Calories: 381.3 | Protein: 15.8g | Carbs: 38.1g | Fat: 18.7g | Fiber: 4.5g

Ingredients:

- Two tbsps. of beans (refried)
- Three tbsps. of salsa
- Three large eggs (beaten)
- One tbsp. of mayonnaise
- Four tortillas (flour)
- One and a half cup of lettuce (shredded)

Method:

1. Combine salsa and beans in a small bowl.

2. Take an iron skillet and heat oil in it. Add the eggs and let the bottom set—Cook for one minute. Spread the mixture of beans on half of the egg and flip one side for making the shape of a half-circle. Cook until the eggs set properly.

3. Spread mayonnaise on the tortillas.

4. Cut the cooked eggs into four equal pieces. Place each piece of eggs on the tortillas. Top with lettuce.

5. Roll the tortillas. Serve hot.

Zucchini Frittata

Total Prep & Cooking Time: Forty minutes

Yields: Five servings

Nutrition Facts: Calories: 258.3 | Protein: 14.2g | Carbs: 9.1g | Fat: 19.6g | Fiber: 3.4g

Ingredients:

- One cup of water
- Three tbsps. of olive oil
- Half tsp. of salt
- Half bell pepper (green, chopped)
- Three zucchinis (cut in slices of half-inch)
- Two garlic cloves (peeled)
- One onion (diced)
- Six mushrooms (chopped)
- One tbsp. of butter
- Five eggs
- Pepper and salt (to taste)
- One and a half cup of mozzarella cheese (shredded)
- Three tbsps. of parmesan cheese

Method:

1. Start by preheating your oven at 160/175 degrees Celsius.

2. Take a large skillet and combine olive oil, water, green pepper, salt, garlic cloves, and zucchini. Simmer the mixture until the zucchini is soft—Cook for seven minutes.

3. Drain the water and remove the garlic; add mushroom, onion, and butter. Keep cooking until the onion turns transparent. Add the eggs and keep stirring. Add pepper and salt for seasoning. Cook until the eggs are firm.

4. Add mozzarella cheese from the top.

5. Bake in the oven for ten minutes.

6. Remove the frittata from the oven and add parmesan cheese from the top. Place under the broiler for about five minutes.

7. Cut the frittata in wedges and serve warm.

Oatmeal And Strawberry Smoothie

Total Prep & Cooking Time: Twenty minutes

Yields: Two servings

Nutrition Facts: Calories: 204.1 | Protein: 5.2g | Carbs: 41.3g | Fat: 2.7g | Fiber: 6.9g

Ingredients:

- One cup of almond milk
- Half cup of rolled oats
- Fourteen strawberries (frozen)
- One banana (cut in chunks)
- Two tsps. of agave nectar
- Half tsp. of vanilla extract

Method:

1. Add almond milk, strawberries, oats, agave nectar, banana, and vanilla extract in a food processor. Keep blending until smooth.
2. Serve with pieces of strawberry from the top.

Chapter 2: Appetizers Recipes

Hosting a party but not sure which appetizers to prepare as most of your guests are vegetarians? No worries as I have included some great vegetarian recipes for appetizers in this section.

Buffalo Cauliflower

Total Prep & Cooking Time: Thirty minutes

Yields: Twelve servings

Nutrition Facts: Calories: 120 | Protein: 4.2g | Carbs: 7.9g | Fat: 8.7g | Fiber: 2.3g

Ingredients

- One serving of cooking spray
- Half cup of buffalo sauce
- Three tbsps. of mayonnaise
- One large egg
- Six cups of cauliflower florets
- Two cups of garlic croutons
- One-fourth cup of parmesan cheese (grated)

For the dipping sauce:

- One-fourth cup of each
    - Sour cream
    - Blue cheese salad dressing
- One tsp. of black pepper (ground)

Method:

1. Start by preheating your oven to 230 degrees Celsius. Use a cooking spray for greasing a baking tray.
2. Combine mayonnaise, buffalo sauce, and egg in a bowl. Toss the florets of cauliflower in the mixture of sauce and coat properly.
3. Spread the tossed florets on the baking tray.
4. Add the croutons on a blender and pulse them into crumbs. Add the cheese and pulse again. Spread the mixture of cheese and croutons over the florets of cauliflower.
5. Bake for fifteen minutes until tender and browned. Allow the florets to sit for five minutes.
6. Mix all the ingredients for the dipping sauce.
7. Serve cauliflower florets with dip sauce by the side.

Garlic Bread And Veggie Delight

Total Prep & Cooking Time: Thirty minutes

Yields: Five servings

Nutrition Facts: Calories: 390.2 | Protein: 12.4g | Carbs: 58.7g | Fat: 11.6g | Fiber: 7.2g

Ingredients:

- One cup of olive oil
- One garlic clove (chopped)
- One eggplant (cubed)
- One zucchini (cubed)
- One tomato (chopped)
- One tsp. of salt
- Two tsps. of each
    - Basil (minced)
    - Oregano (minced)
- One baguette
- Four tsps. of garlic powder
- Six tsps. of butter

Method:

1. Take a large skillet and add olive oil to it. Add garlic and fry for two minutes until browned.

2. Add the zucchini and eggplant to the skillet and cook for five minutes. Make sure that the eggplant is tender and brown.

3. Add the chunks of tomato and combine the veggies; add basil, oregano, and salt. Cook for two minutes and remove from heat.

4. Preheat oven 140/165 degrees Celsius.

5. Slice the baguette into one-inch slices, approximately twelve slices. Add butter and garlic powder on the bread slices and place them on the oven rack. Heat the bread for five minutes.

6. Arrange the heated bread slices on a plate. Top the slices with vegetables.

7. Serve immediately.

Spinach Parmesan Balls

Total Prep & Cooking Time: Thirty minutes

Yields: Ten servings

Nutrition Facts: Calories: 254.1 | Protein: 11.4g | Carbs: 18.4g | Fat: 14.2g | Fiber: 3.5g

Ingredients:

- Twenty ounces of frozen spinach (chopped)
- Two cups of bread crumbs
- One cup of parmesan cheese (grated)
- Half cup of butter (melted)
- Four green onions (chopped)
- Four eggs (beaten)
- Pepper and salt (for seasoning)

Method:

1. Start by preheating your oven at 175 degrees Celsius.
2. Take a bowl and combine spinach, bread crumbs, cheese, green onions, butter, pepper, salt, and eggs. Make balls of one-inch size from the prepared mixture.
3. Arrange the spinach balls on a baking tray. Bake for fifteen minutes until browned.
4. Serve hot.

Cheese Garlic Bread

Total Prep & Cooking Time: Thirty minutes

Yields: Eight servings

Nutrition Facts: Calories: 260 | Protein: 7.1g | Carbs: 29.7g | Fat: 11.4g | Fiber: 1.5g

Ingredients:

- Half cup of butter (melted)
- One tsp. of garlic salt
- One-fourth tsp. of rosemary (dried)
- One-eighth tsp. of each
    - Basil (dried)
    - Thyme (dried)
    - Garlic powder
- One tbsp. of parmesan cheese (grated)
- One loaf of French bread (halved)

Method:

1. Preheat oven at 150 degrees Celsius.
2. Mix garlic salt, butter, basil, rosemary, thyme, garlic powder, and cheese in a bowl.
3. Spread the butter mixture on the halves of the bread. Add extra cheese from the top if you want to.
4. Place halves of bread on a baking tray. Bake for twelve minutes until browned.

Stuffed Mushrooms

Total Prep & Cooking Time: Forty-five minutes

Yields: Twelve servings

Nutrition Facts: Calories: 89 | Protein: 2.6g | Carbs: 1.3g | Fat: 8.9g | Fiber: 0.6g

Ingredients:

- Twelve whole mushrooms
- One tbsp. of each
    - Minced garlic
    - Vegetable oil
- Eight ounces of cream cheese (softened)
- One-fourth cup of parmesan cheese (grated)
- One-fourth tsp. of each
    - Onion powder
    - Black pepper (ground)
    - Cayenne powder (ground)

Method:

1. Preheat the oven to 175 degrees Celsius. Grease a baking tray with the help of cooking spray.

2. Clean the mushrooms using a damp kitchen towel; break the stems. Chop the mushroom stems finely.

3. Take a skillet and heat oil in it. Add chopped stems of mushroom and garlic—Cook for five minutes.

4. Remove the skillet from heat and let it cool. Add the cream cheese, black pepper, parmesan cheese, cayenne powder, and onion powder. Mix well.

5. Use a small spoon for filling the mushroom caps with the mushroom stuffing.

6. Place the mushroom caps on the prepared baking tray.

7. Bake for twenty minutes until liquid forms under the mushroom caps.

Tomato Bruschetta

Total Prep & Cooking Time: Thirty-five minutes

Yields: Twelve servings

Nutrition Facts: Calories: 214.1 | Protein: 10.6g | Carbs: 23.1g | Fat: 8.8g | Fiber: 2.6g

Ingredients:

- Six tomatoes (chopped)
- Half cup of sun-dried tomatoes
- Three garlic cloves (minced)
- One-fourth cup of olive oil
- Two tbsps. of balsamic vinegar
- One-third cup of basil
- One-fourth tsp. of each
    - Black pepper (ground)
    - Salt
- One baguette
- Two cups of mozzarella cheese (shredded)

Method:

1. Preheat your oven on the setting of broiler.

2. Combine tomatoes, olive oil, vinegar, garlic, sun-dried tomatoes, basil, pepper, and salt in a bowl. Let the mixture sit for ten minutes.

3. Cut the baguette into slices of a three-fourth inch. Arrange the baguette slices on a baking tray. Broil for two minutes until browned.

4. Add the mixture of tomatoes on the slices of bread and top with mozzarella cheese.

5. Broil again for five minutes.

Spicy Pumpkin Seeds

Total Prep & Cooking Time: One hour and ten minutes

Yields: Eight servings

Nutrition Facts: Calories: 91 | Protein: 3.2g | Carbs: 8.8g | Fat: 4.9g | Fiber: 0.7g

Ingredients:

- Two tbsps. of margarine
- Half tsp. of salt
- One-eighth tsp. of garlic salt
- Two tsps. of Worcestershire sauce
- Two cups of pumpkin seeds (raw)

Method:

1. Preheat your oven at 135 degrees Celsius.
2. Combine the ingredients in a mixing bowl.
3. Bake for one hour. Stir in between.

Chapter 3: Soups & Side Dishes Recipes

Soup forms an integral part of a vegetarian diet along with the side dishes. Here are some easy vegetarian recipes for side dishes and soups that you can include in your diet.

Carrot Soup
Total Prep & Cooking Time: Forty-five minutes

Yields: Four servings

Nutrition Facts: Calories: 351 | Protein: 3.2g | Carbs: 23.1g | Fat: 29.7g | Fiber: 4.2g

Ingredients:

- Two tbsps. of olive oil
- Four-hundred grams of carrots (cut in disks of half-inch)
- Half onion (diced)

- Four cloves of garlic (smashed)
- Two tsps. of cumin seeds
- Four cups of vegetable stock
- Two bay leaves
- One tsp. of salt
- One-fourth tsp. of white pepper
- Two tsps. of honey
- One-fourth cup of yogurt

Method:

1. Take a heavy bottom pan and add oil in it. Add onions, garlic, and cumin to the pan. Sauté on a medium flame for six minutes until tender and golden in color. Stir occasionally.

2. Add the stock, carrots, salt, bay leaves, white pepper, and simmer the mixture. Cover the pan and simmer for twenty minutes. Allow the soup to cool down for five minutes.

3. Use an immersion blender for blending the soup. Blend until you reach a silky smooth consistency.

4. Return the soup to heat and add honey. Stir the soup. Add yogurt and simmer. Taste the soup and adjust the seasonings. Keep the soup warm on very low flame until you serve.

5. Divide the soup among serving bowls. Serve with a dollop of yogurt from the top.

Note: You can use ground spices in place of the whole spices. But, whole spices will help in adding extra flavor.

Celery Soup

Total Prep & Cooking Time: Thirty-five minutes

Yields: Seven servings

Nutrition Facts: Calories: 180 | Protein: 4.2g | Carbs: 23.1g | Fat: 9.2g | Fiber: 4.9g

Ingredients:

- Two tbsps. of olive oil
- One onion (diced)
- Four cloves of garlic (chopped)
- Six cups of celery (thinly sliced)
- Two cups of potatoes (sliced in rounds)

- Four cups of vegetable stock
- One cup of water
- One bay leaf
- One tsp. of salt
- Half tsp. of pepper
- One-third tsp. of cayenne
- Half cup of sour cream
- One-fourth cup of each
    - Parsley (small stems)
    - Dill (small stems)

Method:

1. Take a large pot and add oil in it. Heat the oil and start adding the onion. Cook for five minutes until golden.

2. Roughly chop celery, potatoes, and garlic. Add garlic and cook the mixture for two minutes. Add potatoes, celery, stock, bay leaf, water, salt, cayenne, and pepper. The liquid needs to be enough to cover the vegetables. Cover the pot and boil the mixture. Simmer for ten minutes.

3. Remove bay leaf after turning off the stove. Add herbs to the pot and allow them to wilt.

4. Take an immersion blender and start blending the soup until silky smooth.

5. Return the pot to heat and cook over low flame for five minutes.

6. Serve with sour cream from the top.

Tomato Soup And Halloumi Croutons

Total Prep & Cooking Time: One hour and five minutes

Yields: Six servings

Nutrition Facts: Calories: 285 | Protein: 10.3g | Carbs: 13.2g | Fat: 23.2g | Fiber: 4.9g

Ingredients:

- Three pounds of tomatoes
- Half red onion (sliced in thin rings)
- Six cloves of garlic
- Two tsps. of thyme leaves

- One-third cup of oil
- Four cups of vegetable stock
- One-fourth cup of basil leaves (chopped)
- One cup of Greek yogurt

For croutons:

- One block of halloumi cheese (cut in cubes of three-fourth inch)
- One tbsp. of oil

Method:

1. Start by preheating your oven at 200 degrees Celsius.

2. Use parchment paper for lining baking sheet. Spread the onions, tomatoes, and garlic on the sheet. Drizzle with some oil from the top—roast in the oven for thirty minutes.

3. Heat some oil in a pan and start adding the halloumi cubes. Cook for four minutes until golden on all sides.

4. Add the roasted veggies in a pot along with the vegetable stock. Use an immersion blender for blending the soup until smooth. Place the pot over a low flame and add seasonings of your choice. Simmer the soup and add basil. Simmer for ten minutes.

5. Add half a cup of yogurt to the soup.

6. Serve the soup in serving bowls with croutons from the top.

Baked Potatoes And Mushrooms With Spinach

Total Prep & Cooking Time: Forty-five minutes

Yields: Four servings

Nutrition Facts: Calories: 235.1 | Protein: 7.1g | Carbs: 27.1g | Fat: 11.3g | Fiber: 4.9g

Ingredients:

- One pound of potatoes (halved)
- Three tbsps. of olive oil
- Half pound of Portobello mushroom
- Six garlic cloves
- Two tbsps. of thyme (chopped)
- One pinch of black pepper and salt
- One-fourth cup of cherry tomatoes
- Half cup of spinach (sliced)
- Two tbsps. of pine nuts (toasted)

Method:

1. Preheat your oven at 200/220 degrees Celsius.

2. Add the potatoes in a roasting pan and drizzle some oil from the top. Roast the potatoes for fifteen minutes.

3. Add mushrooms along with garlic to the pan. Add thyme from the top along with some olive oil. Sprinkle black pepper and salt. Roast again for five minutes.

4. Add cherry tomatoes to the pan. Cook again for five minutes until the mushrooms are tender.

5. Add toasted pine nuts from the top and serve with spinach by the side.

Garlic Potatoes

Total Prep & Cooking Time: Fifty minutes

Yields: Four servings

Nutrition Facts: Calories: 270.2 | Protein: 5.2g | Carbs: 39.7g | Fat: 12.1g | Fiber: 4.9g

Ingredients:

- Two pounds of red potatoes (quartered)
- One-fourth cup of butter (melted)
- Two tsps. of garlic (minced)
- One tsp. of salt
- One lemon (juiced)
- One tbsp. of parmesan cheese (grated)

Method:

1. Start by preheating the oven at 175 degrees Celsius.
2. Place the potatoes in a baking dish.
3. Combine butter, lemon juice, garlic, and salt in a small bowl. Add this mixture over the potatoes and stir for coating. Add parmesan cheese from the top.

4. Bake the potatoes by covering the dish in the preheated oven for thirty minutes. Remove the cover and bake again for ten minutes.

Buttery Carrots

Total Prep & Cooking Time: Twenty-five minutes

Yields: Four servings

Nutrition Facts: Calories: 182.3 | Protein: 0.8g | Carbs: 21.3g | Fat: 10.3g | Fiber: 3.9g

Ingredients:

- One pound of baby carrots
- One-fourth cup of margarine
- One-third cup of brown sugar

Method:

1. Cook the baby carrots in boiling water. Drain most of the liquid leaving behind a little bit of liquid at the base.

2. Remove the carrots from the pot. Add brown sugar along with margarine. Simmer the mixture for two minutes and add the carrots to the pot. Toss well for combining.

3. Serve warm.

Chapter 4: Main Course Recipes

After you are done with the soups and side dishes, now it is time to jump into the main course. Here are some tasty main course recipes that you can include within your vegetarian diet plan.

Nut And Tofu Loaf

Total Prep & Cooking Time: One hour and forty minutes

Yields: Six servings

Nutrition Facts: Calories: 308.3 | Protein: 15.2g | Carbs: 27.6g | Fat: 14.2g | Fiber: 4.8g

Ingredients:

- One serving of cooking spray
- Twelve ounces of tofu (firm, drained, cubed)
- Two large eggs
- One ounce dry mix of onion soup
- One tbsp. of soy sauce
- Three-fourth cup of walnuts (chopped)
- One tsp. of olive oil
- Eight ounces of fresh mushrooms (sliced)
- One onion (chopped)
- Two celery stalks (chopped)
- Two tsps. of oregano (dried)
- One and a half tsps. of basil (dried)
- Half tsp. of sage (dried)
- Two cups of bread crumbs

Method:

1. Start by preheating the oven at 175 degrees Celsius. Use a cooking spray for greasing loaf pan.

2. Place eggs, tofu, soy sauce, and onion soup mix in a blender. Blend the ingredients until properly combined. Add the walnuts and blend again. Transfer the mixture of tofu to a bowl.

3. Take a large skillet and heat oil in it. Add mushrooms and cook them for four minutes. Add celery and cook for two minutes—season with basil, sage, and oregano.

4. Stir bread crumbs and veggies into the mixture of tofu. Press the loaf mixture into the pan.

5. Bake the loaf in the oven for sixty to seventy minutes.

6. Let the loaf cool down for five minutes before serving.

7. Slice the loaf and serve warm.

Velvety Chickpea Curry

Total Prep & Cooking Time: Forty-five minutes

Yields: Six servings

Nutrition Facts: Calories: 408.3 | Protein: 10.2g | Carbs: 68.3g | Fat: 11.2g | Fiber: 8.9g

Ingredients:

- One tbsp. of each
  - Ginger root (minced)
  - Coconut oil
- One onion (sliced)
- Four garlic cloves (minced)
- Two tbsps. of curry powder
- One-fourth tsp. of pepper flakes
- Three cups of vegetable stock
- Two tbsps. of each
  - Soy sauce
  - Tomato paste
  - Maple syrup
- Half pound of potatoes (cut in pieces of a three-fourth inch)
- One carrot (sliced)
- Four cups of cauliflower florets
- One can of chickpeas (rinsed)
- Half cup of coconut milk
- One-fourth cup of cilantro (chopped)
- Half cup of peas (frozen)
- Salt (for seasoning)

Method:

1. Take a heavy-based pot and melt coconut oil in it. Add onions to the pot and sauté for five minutes. Add garlic and ginger to the pot—Cook for thirty seconds. Add pepper flakes, curry powder, soy sauce, stock, tomato paste, and maple syrup. Stir well.

2. Add carrots and potatoes to the pot and cover. Boil the mixture. Slightly open the cover and simmer for ten minutes. Add chickpeas, cauliflower, cilantro, and coconut milk. Stir well for combining. Simmer again for seven minutes. Add peas and cook for one minute.

3. Season with salt and cook for one minute.

4. Serve with basmati rice and cilantro from the top.

Tofu Pad Thai

Total Prep & Cooking Time: Forty-five minutes

Yields: Four servings

Nutrition Facts: Calories: 451 | Protein: 15.4g | Carbs: 60.1g | Fat: 15.2g | Fiber: 4.2g

;

Ingredients

- Twelve ounces of tofu (drained, cubed)
- One tbsp. of cornstarch
- Three tbsps. of vegetable oil
- Eight ounces of rice noodles

For the sauce:

- One-fourth cup of each
    - Sriracha sauce
    - Water
    - Soy sauce
- Two tbsps. of white sugar
- One tbsp. of tamarind concentrate
- One tsp. of pepper flakes
- One large egg
- Two tbsps. of spring onions (chopped)
- One and a half tbsp. of peanuts (crushed)
- One lime (cut in wedges)

Method:

1. Coat the tofu cubes with cornstarch in a large bowl.

2. Heat two tbsps. of oil in a skillet. Fry the coated tofu for two minutes on each side.

3. Place the rice noodles in a medium bowl. Cover the noodles using hot boiling water. Soak the noodles until soft for three minutes. Drain the water.

4. Mix sriracha sauce, water, sugar, soy sauce, pepper flakes, and tamarind concentrate in a skillet. Cook for five minutes.

5. Heat one tbsp. of oil in a large wok. Add noodles, onion, along with the tofu. Cook the mixture for three minutes. Add sauce and toss it for combining.

6. Push the noodles to a side and crack the egg in the center. Stir for thirty seconds and mix with the noodles.

7. Serve with peanuts, green onion, and wedges of lime.

Eggplant Parmesan

Total Prep & Cooking Time: One hour

Yields: Ten servings

Nutrition Facts: Calories: 480.2 | Protein: 21.2g | Carbs: 60.1g | Fat: 15.2g | Fiber: 9.8g

Ingredients:

- Three eggplants (sliced)
- Two eggs (beaten)
- Four cups of bread crumbs
- Six cups of spaghetti sauce
- Sixteen ounces of mozzarella cheese (shredded)
- Half cup of parmesan cheese
- Half tsp. of basil (dried)

Method:

1. Preheat the oven at 175 degrees Celsius.
2. Dip the slices of eggplant in egg and then coat in bread crumbs.
3. Arrange the slices of eggplant in a baking sheet and bake for five minutes on both sides.
4. Take a baking dish and spread the spaghetti sauce for covering the base. Arrange the eggplant slices over the sauce. Sprinkle cheese from the top. Repeat for the remaining layers. Top with basil and cheese.
5. Bake for thirty-minutes until browned.

Veg Korma

Total Prep & Cooking Time: Fifty-five minutes

Yields: Four servings

Nutrition Facts: Calories: 451 | Protein: 8.4g | Carbs: 40.1g | Fat: 30.2g | Fiber: 8.7g

Ingredients:

- Two tbsps. of vegetable oil
- One onion (diced)
- One tsp. of ginger root (minced)
- Four garlic cloves (minced)
- Two potatoes (cubed)
- Four carrots (cubed)
- One jalapeno pepper (sliced)
- Three tbsps. of cashews (ground)
- One can of tomato sauce
- Two tsps. of salt
- One and a half tbsps. of curry powder
- One cup of green peas (frozen)
- One red bell pepper (roughly chopped)
- One-third yellow bell pepper (roughly chopped)
- One bunch of cilantro
- Half cup of heavy cream

Method:

1. Take a skillet and heat oil in it. Add onions to the oil and cook until soft. Add garlic and ginger to the skillet. Cook for one minute. Add carrots, potatoes, cashews, jalapenos, and tomato sauce. Add curry powder and season with salt. Stir well and cook for ten minutes until the potatoes are soft.

2. Add bell pepper, peas, and cream. Lower the flame and cover the skillet—Cook for ten minutes.

3. Serve with cilantro from the top.

Mac And Cheese

Total Prep & Cooking Time: Fifty minutes

Yields: Six servings

Nutrition Facts: Calories: 456 | Protein: 24g | Carbs: 33.1g | Fat: 24.9g | Fiber: 2.3g

Ingredients:

- Two cups of elbow macaroni (uncooked)
- One-fourth cup of butter
- Two tbsps. of flour
- One tsp. of each
  - Black pepper (ground)
  - Mustard powder
- Two cups of milk
- Eight ounces of each
  - Cheese food (cubed)
  - American cheese (cubed)
- Half cup of bread crumbs

Method:

1. Preheat the oven at 180/200 degrees Celsius. Take a casserole dish and grease with butter.

2. Boil water in a pot with salt. Add the pasta and cook the pasta for six minutes. Drain the water.

3. Take a saucepan. Melt butter in it. Add mustard powder, flour, and pepper. Add milk and stir constantly. Add the cheeses and mix for two minutes until the sauce thickens.

4. Add the macaroni to the cheese mixture. Mix well.

5. Transfer the pasta mixture to the greased dish. Add bread crumbs from the top.

6. Bake for twenty minutes by covering the dish.

7. Serve hot.

Sesame Noodles

Total Prep & Cooking Time: Thirty minutes   Yields: Eight servings

Nutrition Facts: Calories: 365.2 | Protein: 7.3g | Carbs: 51.1g | Fat: 13.2g | Fiber: 3.9g

Ingredients:

- Sixteen ounces of linguine pasta
- Six garlic cloves (minced)
- Six tbsps. of each
    - Safflower oil
    - Sugar
    - Rice vinegar
    - Soy sauce
- Two tsps. of chili sauce
- Two tbsps. of sesame oil
- Six green onions (sliced)
- One tsp. of sesame seeds (toasted)

Method:

1. Boil water in a large pot along with some salt. Add the pasta. Keep cooking for eight minutes. Drain all the water.
2. Take a saucepan and heat oil in it. Add garlic, sugar, soy sauce, chili sauce, and sesame oil. Boil the mixture until the sugar gets dissolved.
3. Add the sauce to the cooked pasta and toss well for combining.
4. Serve with sesame seeds and green onions from the top.

Chapter 5: Dessert Recipes

Having a great dessert after a tasty meal can make you, as well as your stomach, feel good. So, here are some vegetarian dessert recipes for you.

Raspberry And Rosewater Sponge Cake

Total Prep & Cooking Time: Fifty-five minutes

Yields: Ten servings

Nutrition Facts: Calories: 441 | Protein: 4.1g | Carbs: 51.3g | Fat: 23.1g | Fiber: 1.3g

Ingredients:

- Two-hundred grams of butter (softened)
- Two-hundred and fifty grams of caster sugar
- Four eggs (beaten)
- One tsp. of vanilla extract
- Two cups of flour

For the rose filling:

- Half cup of double cream
- One tsp. of rosewater
- Four tbsps. of raspberry jam
- One-third cup of raspberries (crushed)

For rose icing:

- Half cup of icing sugar
- Half tsp. of rosewater

Method:

1. Heat the oven at 160 degrees Celsius.

2. Use parchment paper for lining two baking tins—grease with butter.

3. Mix sugar and butter in a bowl. Add the eggs and mix again.

4. Add vanilla extract to the egg mixture and mix. Add flour and fold.

5. Divide the cake batter into the prepared baking tins and bake in the oven for twenty minutes. Let the cakes cool for ten minutes.

6. Whisk double cream along with rosewater. Add the jam and mix.

7. Place one of the cakes on a serving plate and add the cream mixture. Add raspberries from the top and place the other cake on top.

8. Mix all the ingredients for the icing.

9. Serve the cake with rose icing from the top.

Easy Tiramisu

Total Prep & Cooking Time: One hour and fifteen minutes

Yields: Two servings

Nutrition Facts: Calories: 741 | Protein: 11.3g | Carbs: 44.3g | Fat: 51.6g | Fiber: 1.9g

Ingredients:

- Three tsps. of coffee granules
- Three tbsps. of coffee liqueur
- One and a half cup of mascarpone
- Half cup of condensed milk
- Six sponge fingers
- One tbsp. of cocoa powder

Method:

1. Mix coffee granules in two tbsps. of boiling water and stir for combining. Add three tbsps. of cold water along with coffee liqueur. Pour the mixture in a dish and keep aside.

2. Beat condensed milk, mascarpone, and vanilla extract in a bowl using a hand blender.

3. Break the fingers into two pieces and soak them in the mixture of coffee for thirty seconds.

4. Take a sundae glass and add the sponge fingers at the base. Add the cream mixture on top. Sift cocoa powder and chill in the refrigerator for one hour.

Chocolate Marquise

Total Prep & Cooking Time: Two hours and fifty-five minutes

Yields: Ten servings

Nutrition Facts: Calories: 710.3 | Protein: 7.8g | Carbs: 59.8g | Fat: 53g | Fiber: 1.5g

Ingredients:

- Three-hundred grams of dark chocolate
- Half cup of each
    - Caster sugar
    - Butter (softened)
- Six tbsps. of cocoa powder
- Six eggs
- One-third cup of double cream
- One-fourth cup of mint chocolate

Method:

1. Break the dark chocolate in small pieces and melt it using a double boiler system.
2. Beat butter and sugar in a bowl until creamy.

3. Separate the egg whites and yolks.

4. Mix the yolks with the sugar mixture until creamy.

5. Whip the double cream in another bowl.

6. Add the melted chocolate in the mixture of butter and fold gently. Add the whipped cream and mix well.

7. Spoon the mixture of chocolate in a piping bag.

8. Take a baking tin and pipe one layer of chocolate at the base of the tin. Cover the tin with pieces of mint chocolate. Repeat for the other layers. You will need to make four layers of mint chocolate.

9. Cover the tin with a cling film.

10. Chill the marquise in the fridge for two hours.

11. Remove the marquise from the tin by using a sharp knife.

12. Serve by cutting into slices.

Lemon Syllabub

Total Prep & Cooking Time: Fifteen minutes

Yields: Four servings

Nutrition Facts: Calories: 328 | Protein: 2.2g | Carbs: 14.6g | Fat: 28.6g | Fiber: 0.2g

Ingredients:

- Two cups of whipping cream
- Half cup of caster sugar
- Three tbsps. of white wine
- Half a lemon (juice and zest)
- Berries (for serving)

Method:

1. Mix sugar and whipping cream in a bowl. Whip until soft peaks are formed.
2. Add white wine in the mixture. Mix well. Add lemon juice and lemon zest in the mixture. Combine the ingredients properly.
3. Spoon the mixture into serving bowls or glasses.
4. Sprinkle remaining lemon zest from the top.
5. Serve the lemon syllabub with berries.

Note: You can use a mix of berries or only one type of berry.

PART IV

Smoothie Diet Recipes

The smoothie diet is all about replacing some of your meals with smoothies that are loaded with veggies and fruits. It has been found that the smoothie diet is very helpful in losing weight along with excess fat. The ingredients of the smoothies will vary, but they will focus mainly on vegetables and fruits. The best part about the smoothie diet is that there is no need to count your calorie intake and less food tracking. The diet is very low in calories and is also loaded with phytonutrients.

Apart from weight loss, there are various other benefits of the smoothie diet. It can help you to stay full for a longer time as most smoothies are rich in fiber. It can also help you to control your cravings as smoothies are full of flavor and nutrients. Whenever you feel like snacking, just prepare a smoothie, and you are good to go. Also, smoothies can aid in digestion as they are rich in important minerals and vitamins. Fruits such as mango are rich in carotenoids that can help in improving your skin quality. As the smoothie diet is mainly based on veggies and fruits, it can detoxify your body.

In this section, you will find various recipes of smoothies that you can include in your smoothie diet.

Chapter 1: Fruit Smoothies

The best way of having fruits is by making smoothies. Fruit smoothies can help you start your day with loads of nutrients so that you can remain energetic throughout the day. Here are some easy-to-make fruit smoothie recipes that you can enjoy during any time of the day.

Quick Fruit Smoothie

Total Prep & Cooking Time: Fifteen minutes

Yields: Four servings

Nutrition Facts: Calories: 115.2 | Protein: 1.2g | Carbs: 27.2g | Fat: 0.5g | Fiber: 3.6g

Ingredients

- One cup of strawberries
- One banana (cut in chunks)
- Two peaches
- Two cups of ice
- One cup of orange and mango juice

Method:

1. Add banana, strawberries, and peaches in a blender.
2. Blend until frothy and smooth.
3. Add the orange and mango juice and blend again. Add ice for adjusting the consistency and blend for two minutes.
4. Divide the smoothie in glasses and serve with mango chunks from the top.

Triple Threat Smoothie

Total Prep & Cooking Time: Ten minutes

Yields: Four servings

Nutrition Facts: Calories: 132.2 | Protein: 3.4g | Carbs: 27.6g | Fat: 1.3g | Fiber: 2.7g

Ingredients

- One kiwi (sliced)
- One banana (chopped)
- One cup of each
    - Ice cubes
    - Strawberries
- Half cup of blueberries
- One-third cup of orange juice
- Eight ounces of peach yogurt

Method:

1. Add kiwi, strawberries, and bananas in a food processor.
2. Blend until smooth.
3. Add the blueberries along with orange juice. Blend again for two minutes.
4. Add peach yogurt and ice cubes. Give it a pulse.
5. Pour the prepared smoothie in smoothie glasses and serve with blueberry chunks from the top.

Tropical Smoothie

Total Prep & Cooking Time: Fifteen minutes

Yields: Two servings

Nutrition Facts: Calories: 127.3 | Protein: 1.6g | Carbs: 30.5g | Fat: 0.7g | Fiber: 4.2g

Ingredients

- One mango (seeded)
- One papaya (cubed)
- Half cup of strawberries
- One-third cup of orange juice
- Five ice cubes

Method:

1. Add mango, strawberries, and papaya in a blender. Blend the ingredients until smooth.
2. Add ice cubes and orange juice for adjusting the consistency.
3. Blend again.
4. Serve with strawberry chunks from the top.

Fruit and Mint Smoothie

Total Prep & Cooking Time: Fifteen minutes

Yields: Two servings

Nutrition Facts: Calories: 90.3 | Protein: 0.7g | Carbs: 21.4g | Fat: 0.4g | Fiber: 2.5g

Ingredients

- One-fourth cup of each
  - Applesauce (unsweetened)
  - Red grapes (seedless, frozen)
- One tbsp. of lime juice
- Three strawberries (frozen)
- One cup of pineapple cubes
- Three mint leaves

Method:

1. Add grapes, lime juice, and applesauce in a blender. Blend the ingredients until frothy and smooth.

2. Add pineapple cubes, mint leaves, and frozen strawberries in the blender. Pulse the ingredients for a few times until the pineapple and strawberries are crushed.

3. Serve with mint leaves from the top.

Banana Smoothie

Total Prep & Cooking Time: Ten minutes

Yields: Four servings

Nutrition Facts: Calories: 122.6 | Protein: 1.3g | Carbs: 34.6g | Fat: 0.4g | Fiber: 2.2g

Ingredients

- Three bananas (sliced)
- One cup of fresh pineapple juice
- One tbsp. of honey
- Eight cubes of ice

Method:

1. Combine the bananas and pineapple juice in a blender.
2. Blend until smooth.
3. Add ice cubes along with honey.
4. Blend for two minutes.
5. Serve immediately.

Dragon Fruit Smoothie

Total Prep & Cooking Time: Twenty minutes

Yields: Four servings

Nutrition Facts: Calories: 147.6 | Protein: 5.2g | Carbs: 21.4g | Fat: 6.4g | Fiber: 2.9g

Ingredients

- One-fourth cup of almonds
- Two tbsps. of shredded coconut
- One tsp. of chocolate chips
- One cup of yogurt
- One dragon fruit (chopped)
- Half cup of pineapple cubes
- One tbsp. of honey

Method:

1. Add almonds, dragon fruit, coconut, and chocolate chips in a high power blender. Blend until smooth.

2. Add yogurt, pineapple, and honey. Blend well.

3. Serve with chunks of dragon fruit from the top.

Kefir Blueberry Smoothie

Total Prep & Cooking Time: Fifteen minutes

Yields: Two servings

Nutrition Facts: Calories: 304.2 | Protein: 7.3g | Carbs: 41.3g | Fat: 13.2g | Fiber: 4.6g

Ingredients

- Half cup of kefir
- One cup of blueberries (frozen)
- Half banana (cubed)

- One tbsp. of almond butter
- Two tsps. of honey

Method:

1. Add blueberries, banana cubes, and kefir in a blender.
2. Blend until smooth.
3. Add honey and almond butter.
4. Pulse the smoothie for a few times.
5. Serve immediately.

Ginger Fruit Smoothie

Total Prep & Cooking Time: Fifteen minutes

Yields: Two servings

Nutrition Facts: Calories: 160.2 | Protein: 1.9g | Carbs: 41.3g | Fat: 0.7g | Fiber: 5.6g

Ingredients

- One-fourth cup of each
    - Blueberries (frozen)
    - Green grapes (seedless)
- Half cup of green apple (chopped)
- One cup of water
- Three strawberries
- One piece of ginger
- One tbsp. of agave nectar

Method:

1. Add blueberries, grapes, and water in a blender. Blend the ingredients.
2. Add green apple, strawberries, agave nectar, and ginger. Blend for making thick slushy.
3. Serve immediately.

Fruit Batido

Total Prep & Cooking Time: Fifteen minutes

Yields: Six servings

Nutrition Facts: Calories: 129.3 | Protein: 4.2g | Carbs: 17.6g | Fat: 4.6g | Fiber: 0.6g

Ingredients

- One can of evaporated milk
- One cup of papaya (chopped)
- One-fourth cup of white sugar
- One tsp. of vanilla extract
- One tsp. of cinnamon (ground)
- One tray of ice cubes

Method:

1. Add papaya, white sugar, cinnamon, and vanilla extract in a food processor. Blend the ingredients until smooth.
2. Add milk and ice cubes. Blend for making slushy.
3. Serve immediately.

Banana Peanut Butter Smoothie

Total Prep & Cooking Time: Ten minutes

Yields: Four servings

Nutrition Facts: Calories: 332 | Protein: 13.2g | Carbs: 35.3g | Fat: 17.8g | Fiber: 3.9g

Ingredients

- Two bananas (cubed)
- Two cups of milk
- Half cup of peanut butter
- Two tbsps. of honey
- Two cups of ice cubes

Method:

1. Add banana cubes and peanut butter in a blender. Blend for making a smooth paste.
2. Add milk, ice cubes, and honey. Blend the ingredients until smooth.
3. Serve with banana chunks from the top.

Chapter 2: Breakfast Smoothies

Smoothie forms an essential part of breakfast in the smoothie diet plan. Here are some breakfast smoothie recipes for you that can be included in your daily breakfast plan.

Berry Banana Smoothie
Total Prep & Cooking Time: Twenty minutes

Yields: Two servings

Nutrition Facts: Calories: 330 | Protein: 6.7g | Carbs: 56.3g | Fat: 13.2g | Fiber: 5.5g

Ingredients

- One cup of each
    - Strawberries
    - Peaches (cubed)
    - Apples (cubed)
- One banana (cubed)
- Two cups of vanilla ice cream
- Half cup of ice cubes
- One-third cup of milk

Method:

1. Place strawberries, peaches, banana, and apples in a blender. Pulse the ingredients.
2. Add milk, ice cream, and ice cubes. Blend the smoothie until frothy and smooth.
3. Serve with a scoop of ice cream from the top.

Berry Surprise

Total Prep & Cooking Time: Ten minutes

Yields: Two servings

Nutrition Facts: Calories: 164.2 | Protein: 1.2g | Carbs: 40.2g | Fat: 0.4g | Fiber: 4.8g

Ingredients

- One cup of strawberries
- Half cup of pineapple cubes
- One-third cup of raspberries
- Two tbsps. of limeade concentrate (frozen)

Method:

1. Combine pineapple cubes, strawberries, and raspberries in a food processor. Blend the ingredients until smooth.//
2. Add the frozen limeade and blend again.
3. Divide the smoothie in glasses and serve immediately.

Coconut Matcha Smoothie

Total Prep & Cooking Time: Twenty minutes

Yields: Two servings

Nutrition Facts: Calories: 362 | Protein: 7.2g | Carbs: 70.1g | Fat: 8.7g | Fiber: 12.1g

Ingredients

- One large banana
- One cup of frozen mango cubes
- Two leaves of kale (torn)
- Three tbsps. of white beans (drained)
- Two tbsps. of shredded coconut (unsweetened)
- Half tsp. of matcha green tea (powder)
- Half cup of water

Method:

1. Add cubes of mango, banana, white beans, and kale in a blender. Blend all the ingredients until frothy and smooth.

2. Add shredded coconut, white beans, water, and green tea powder. Blend for thirty seconds.

3. Serve with shredded coconut from the top.

Cantaloupe Frenzy

Total Prep & Cooking Time: Ten minutes

Yields: Three servings

Nutrition Facts: Calories: 108.3 | Protein: 1.6g | Carbs: 26.2g | Fat: 0.2g | Fiber: 1.6g

Ingredients

- One cantaloupe (seeded, chopped)
- Three tbsps. of white sugar
- Two cups of ice cubes

Method:

1. Place the chopped cantaloupe along with white sugar in a blender. Puree the mixture.
2. Add cubes of ice and blend again.
3. Pour the smoothie in serving glasses. Serve immediately.

Berry Lemon Smoothie

Total Prep & Cooking Time: Ten minutes

Yields: Four servings

Nutrition Facts: Calories: 97.2 | Protein: 5.4g | Carbs: 19.4g | Fat: 0.4g | Fiber: 1.8g

Ingredients

- Eight ounces of blueberry yogurt
- One and a half cup of milk (skim)
- One cup of ice cubes
- Half cup of blueberries
- One-third cup of strawberries
- One tsp. of lemonade mix

Method:

1. Add blueberry yogurt, skim milk, blueberries, and strawberries in a food processor. Blend the ingredients until smooth.

2. Add lemonade mix and ice cubes. Pulse the mixture for making a creamy and smooth smoothie.

3. Divide the smoothie in glasses and serve.

Orange Glorious

Total Prep & Cooking Time: Ten minutes

Yields: Four servings

Nutrition Facts: Calories: 212 | Protein: 3.4g | Carbs: 47.3g | Fat: 1.5g | Fiber: 0.5g

Ingredients

- Six ounces of orange juice concentrate (frozen)
- One cup of each
    - Water
    - Milk
- Half cup of white sugar
- Twelve ice cubes
- One tsp. of vanilla extract

Method:

1. Combine orange juice concentrate, white sugar, milk, and water in a blender.
2. Add vanilla extract and ice cubes. Blend the mixture until smooth.
3. Pour the smoothie in glasses and enjoy!

Grapefruit Smoothie

Total Prep & Cooking Time: Ten minutes

Yields: Two servings

Nutrition Facts: Calories: 200.3 | Protein: 4.7g | Carbs: 46.3g | Fat: 1.2g | Fiber: 7.6g

Ingredients

- Three grapefruits (peeled)
- One cup of water
- Three ounces of spinach
- Six ice cubes
- Half-inch piece of ginger
- One tsp. of flax seeds

Method:

1. Combine spinach, grapefruit, and ginger in a high power blender. Blend until smooth.
2. Add water, flax seeds, and ice cubes. Blend smooth.
3. Pour the smoothie in glasses and serve.

Sour Smoothie

Total Prep & Cooking Time: Ten minutes

Yields: Two servings

Nutrition Facts: Calories: 102.6 | Protein: 2.3g | Carbs: 30.2g | Fat: 0.7g | Fiber: 7.9g

Ingredients

- One cup of ice cubes
- Two fruit limes (peeled)
- One orange (peeled)
- One lemon (peeled)
- One kiwi (peeled)
- One tsp. of honey

Method:

1. Add fruit limes, lemon, orange, and kiwi in a food processor. Blend until frothy and smooth.
2. Add cubes of ice and honey. Pulse the ingredients.
3. Divide the smoothie in glasses and enjoy!

Ginger Orange Smoothie

Total Prep & Cooking Time: Ten minutes

Yields: One serving

Nutrition Facts: Calories: 115.6 | Protein: 2.2g | Carbs: 27.6g | Fat: 1.3g | Fiber: 5.7g

Ingredients

- One large orange
- Two carrots (peeled, cut in chunks)
- Half cup of each
    - Red grapes
    - Ice cubes
- One-fourth cup of water
- One-inch piece of ginger

Method:

1. Combine carrots, grapes, and orange in a high power blender. Blend until frothy and smooth.
2. Add ice cubes, ginger, and water. Blend the ingredients for thirty seconds.
3. Serve immediately.

Cranberry Smoothie

Total Prep & Cooking Time: One hour and ten minutes

Yields: Two servings

Nutrition Facts: Calories: 155.9 | Protein: 2.2g | Carbs: 33.8g | Fat: 1.6g | Fiber: 5.2g

Ingredients

- One cup of almond milk
- Half cup of mixed berries (frozen)
- One-third cup of cranberries
- One banana

Method:

1. Blend mixed berries, banana, and cranberries in a high power food processor. Blend until smooth.
2. Add almond milk and blend again for twenty seconds.
3. Refrigerate the prepared smoothie for one hour.
4. Serve chilled.

Creamsicle Smoothie

Total Prep & Cooking Time: Ten minutes

Yields: Two servings

Nutrition Facts: Calories: 121.3 | Protein: 4.7g | Carbs: 19.8g | Fat: 2.5g | Fiber: 0.3g

Ingredients

- One cup of orange juice
- One and a half cup of crushed ice
- Half cup of milk
- One tsp. of white sugar

Method:

1. Blend milk, orange juice, white sugar, and ice in a high power blender.
2. Keep blending until there is no large chunk of ice. Try to keep the consistency of slushy.
3. Serve immediately.

Sunshine Smoothie

Total Prep & Cooking Time: Thirty minutes

Yields: Four servings

Nutrition Facts: Calories: 176.8 | Protein: 4.2g | Carbs: 39.9g | Fat: 1.3g | Fiber: 3.9g

Ingredients

- Two nectarines (pitted, quartered)
- One banana (cut in chunks)
- One orange (peeled, quartered)
- One cup of vanilla yogurt
- One-third cup of orange juice
- One tbsp. of honey

Method:

1. Add banana chunks, nectarines, and orange in a blender. Blender for two minutes.
2. Add vanilla yogurt, honey, and orange juice. Blend the ingredients until frothy and smooth.
3. Pour the smoothie in glasses and serve.

Chapter 3: Vegetable Smoothies

Apart from fruit smoothies, vegetable smoothies can also provide you with essential nutrients. In fact, vegetable smoothies are tasty as well. So, here are some vegetable smoothie recipes for you.

Mango Kale Berry Smoothie
Total Prep & Cooking Time: Ten minutes

Yields: Four servings

Nutrition Facts: Calories: 117.3 | Protein: 3.1g | Carbs: 22.6g | Fat: 3.6g | Fiber: 6.2g

Ingredients

- One cup of orange juice
- One-third cup of kale
- One and a half cup of mixed berries (frozen)
- Half cup of mango chunks
- One-fourth cup of water
- Two tbsps. of chia seeds

Method:

1. Take a high power blender and add kale, orange juice, berries, mango chunks, chia seeds, and half a cup of water.
2. Blend the ingredients on high settings until smooth.
3. In case the smoothie is very thick, you can adjust the consistency by adding more water.
4. Pour the smoothie in glasses and serve.

Breakfast Pink Smoothie

Total Prep & Cooking Time: Ten minutes

Yields: Two servings

Nutrition Facts: Calories: 198.3 | Protein: 12.3g | Carbs: 6.3g | Fat: 4.5g | Fiber: 8.8g

Ingredients

- One and a half cup of strawberries (frozen)
- One cup of raspberries
- One orange (peeled)

- Two carrots
- Two cups of coconut milk (light)
- One small beet (quartered)

Method:

1. Add strawberries, raspberries, and orange in a blender. Blend until frothy and smooth.

2. Add beet, carrots, and coconut milk.

3. Blend again for one minute.

4. Divide the smoothie in glasses and serve.

Butternut Squash Smoothie

Total Prep & Cooking Time: Five minutes

Yields: Four servings

Nutrition Facts: Calories: 127.3 | Protein: 2.3g | Carbs: 32.1g | Fat: 1.2g | Fiber: 0.6g

Ingredients

- Two cups of almond milk
- One-fourth cup of nut butter (of your choice)
- One cup of water
- One and a half cup of butternut squash (frozen)
- Two ripe bananas
- One tsp. of cinnamon (ground)
- Two tbsps. of hemp protein
- Half cup of strawberries
- One tbsp. of chia seeds
- Half tbsp. of bee pollen

Method:

1. Add butternut squash, bananas, strawberries, and almond milk in a blender. Blend until frothy and smooth.
2. Add water, nut butter, cinnamon, hemp protein, chia seeds, and bee pollen. Blend the ingredients f0r two minutes.
3. Divide the smoothie in glasses and enjoy!

Zucchini and Wild Blueberry Smoothie

Total Prep & Cooking Time: Ten minutes

Yields: Three servings

Nutrition Facts: Calories: 190.2 | Protein: 7.3g | Carbs: 27.6g | Fat: 8.1g | Fiber: 5.7g

Ingredients

- One banana
- One cup of wild blueberries (frozen)
- One-fourth cup of peas (frozen)
- Half cup of zucchini (frozen, chopped)
- One tbsp. of each
    - Hemp hearts
    - Chia seeds
    - Bee pollen
- One-third cup of almond milk
- Two tbsps. of nut butter (of your choice)
- Ten cubes of ice

Method:

1. Add blueberries, banana, peas, and zucchini in a high power blender. Blend the ingredients for two minutes.

2. Add chia seeds, hemp hearts, almond milk, bee pollen, nut butter, and ice. Blend the mixture for making a thick and smooth smoothie.

3. Pour the smoothie in glasses and serve with chopped blueberries from the top.

Cauliflower and Blueberry Smoothie

Total Prep & Cooking Time: Five minutes

Yields: Two servings

Nutrition Facts: Calories: 201.9 | Protein: 7.1g | Carbs: 32.9g | Fat: 10.3g | Fiber: 4.6g

Ingredients

- One Clementine (peeled)
- Three-fourth cup of cauliflower (frozen)
- Half cup of wild blueberries (frozen)
- One cup of Greek yogurt
- One tbsp. of peanut butter
- Bunch of spinach

Method:

1. Add cauliflower, Clementine, and blueberries in a blender. Blend for one minute.
2. Add peanut butter, spinach, and yogurt. Pulse the ingredients for two minutes until smooth.
3. Divide the prepared smoothie in glasses and enjoy!

Immunity Booster Smoothie

Total Prep & Cooking Time: Ten minutes

Yields: Two servings

Nutrition Facts: Calories: 301.9 | Protein: 5.4g | Carbs: 70.7g | Fat: 4.3g | Fiber: 8.9g

Ingredients

For the orange layer:

- One persimmon (quartered)
- One ripe mango (chopped)
- One lime (juiced)
- One tbsp. of nut butter (of your choice)
- Half tsp. of turmeric powder
- One pinch of cayenne pepper
- One cup of coconut milk

For the pink layer:

- One small beet (cubed)
- One cup of berries (frozen)
- One pink grapefruit (quartered)
- One-fourth cup of pomegranate juice
- Half cup of water
- Six leaves of mint
- One tsp. of honey

Method:

1. Add the ingredients for the orange layer in a blender. Blend for making a smooth liquid.
2. Pour the orange liquid evenly in serving glasses.
3. Add the pink layer ingredients in a blender. Blend for making a smooth liquid.
4. Pour the pink liquid slowly over the orange layer.
5. Pour in such a way so that both layers can be differentiated.
6. Serve immediately.

Ginger, Carrot, and Turmeric Smoothie

Total Prep & Cooking Time: Forty minutes

Yields: Two servings

Nutrition Facts: Calories: 140 | Protein: 2.6g | Carbs: 30.2g | Fat: 2.2g | Fiber: 5.6g

Ingredients

For carrot juice:

- Two cups of water
- Two and a half cups of carrots

For smoothie:

- One ripe banana (sliced)
- One cup of pineapple (frozen, cubed)
- Half tbsp. of ginger
- One-fourth tsp. of turmeric (ground)
- Half cup of carrot juice
- One tbsp. of lemon juice
- One-third cup of almond milk

Method:

1. Add water and carrots in a high power blender. Blend on high settings for making smooth juice.
2. Take a dish towel and strain the juice over a bowl. Squeeze the towel for taking out most of the juice.
3. Add the ingredients for the smoothie in a blender and blend until frothy and creamy.
4. Add carrot juice and blend again.
5. Pour the smoothie in glasses and serve.

Romaine Mango Smoothie

Total Prep & Cooking Time: Five minutes

Yields: Two servings

Nutrition Facts: Calories: 117.3 | Protein: 2.6g | Carbs: 30.2g | Fat: 0.9g | Fiber: 4.2g

Ingredients

- Sixteen ounces of coconut water
- Two mangoes (pitted)
- One head of romaine (chopped)
- One banana
- One orange (peeled)
- Two cups of ice

Method:

1. Add mango, romaine, orange, and banana in a high power blender. Blend the ingredients until frothy and smooth.
2. Add coconut water and ice cubes. Blend for one minute.
3. Pour the prepared smoothie in glasses and serve.

Fig Zucchini Smoothie
Total Prep & Cooking Time: Ten minutes

Yields: Two servings

Nutrition Facts: Calories: 243.3 | Protein: 14.4g | Carbs: 74.3g | Fat: 27.6g | Fiber: 9.3g

Ingredients

- Half cup of cashew nuts
- One tsp. of cinnamon (ground)
- Two figs (halved)
- One banana
- Half tsp. of ginger (minced)
- One-third tsp. of honey
- One-fourth cup of ice cubes
- One pinch of salt
- Two tsps. of vanilla extract
- Three-fourth cup of water
- One cup of zucchini (chopped)

Method:

1. Add all the listed ingredients in a high power blender. Blend for two minutes until creamy and smooth.

2. Pour the smoothie in serving glasses and serve.

Carrot Peach Smoothie

Total Prep & Cooking Time: Ten minutes

Yields: Two servings

Nutrition Facts: Calories: 191.2 | Protein: 11.2g | Carbs: 34.6g | Fat: 2.7g | Fiber: 5.4g

Ingredients

- Two cups of peach
- One cup of baby carrots
- One banana (frozen)
- Two tbsps. of Greek yogurt
- One and a half cup of coconut water
- One tbsp. of honey

Method:

1. Add peach, baby carrots, and banana in a high power blender. Blend on high settings for one minute.

2. Add Greek yogurt, honey, and coconut water. Give the mixture a whizz.

3. Pour the smoothie in glasses and serve.

Sweet Potato and Mango Smoothie

Total Prep & Cooking Time: Ten minutes

Yields: Two servings

Nutrition Facts: Calories: 133.3 | Protein: 3.6g | Carbs: 28.6g | Fat: 1.3g | Fiber: 6.2g

Ingredients

- One small sweet potato (cooked, smashed)
- Half cup of mango chunks (frozen)
- Two cups of coconut milk
- One tbsp. of chia seeds
- Two tsps. of maple syrup
- A handful of ice cubes

Method:

1. Add mango chunks and sweet potato in a high power blender. Blend until frothy and smooth.
2. Add chia seeds, coconut milk, ice cubes, and maple syrup. Blend again for one minute.
3. Divide the smoothie in glasses and serve.

Carrot Cake Smoothie

Total Prep & Cooking Time: Ten minutes

Yields: Two servings

Nutrition Facts: Calories: 289.3 | Protein: 3.6g | Carbs: 47.8g | Fat: 1.3g | Fiber: 0.6g

Ingredients

- One cup of carrots (chopped)
- One banana
- Half cup of almond milk
- One cup of Greek yogurt
- One tbsp. of maple syrup
- One tsp. of cinnamon (ground)
- One-fourth tsp. of nutmeg
- Half tsp. of ginger (ground)
- A handful of ice cubes

Method

1. Add banana, carrots, and almond milk in a blender. Blend until frothy and smooth.

2. Add yogurt, cinnamon, maple syrup, ginger, nutmeg, and ice cubes. Blend again for two minutes.

3. Divide the smoothie in serving glasses and serve.

Notes:

- You can add more ice cubes and turn the smoothie into slushy.
- You can store the leftover smoothie in the freezer for two days.

Chapter 4: Green Smoothies

Green smoothies can help in the process of detoxification as well as weight loss. Here are some easy-to-make green smoothie recipes for you.

Kale Avocado Smoothie

Total Prep & Cooking Time: Ten minutes

Yields: Two servings

Nutrition Facts: Calories: 401 | Protein: 11.2g | Carbs: 64.6g | Fat: 17.3g | Fiber: 10.2g

Ingredients

- One banana (cut in chunks)
- Half cup of blueberry yogurt
- One cup of kale (chopped)
- Half ripe avocado
- One-third cup of almond milk

Method:

1. Add blueberry, banana, avocado, and kale in a blender. Blend for making a smooth mixture.

2. Add the almond milk and blend again.

3. Divide the smoothie in glasses and serve.

Celery Pineapple Smoothie

Total Prep & Cooking Time: Ten minutes

Yields: Two servings

Nutrition Facts: Calories: 112 | Protein: 2.3g | Carbs: 3.6g | Fat: 1.2g | Fiber: 3.9g

Ingredients

- Three celery stalks (chopped)
- One cup of cubed pineapple
- One banana
- One pear
- Half cup of almond milk
- One tsp. of honey

Method:

1. Add celery stalks, pear, banana, and cubes of pineapple in a food processor. Blend until frothy and smooth.
2. Add honey and almond milk. Blend for two minutes.
3. Pour the smoothie in serving glasses and enjoy!

Cucumber Mango and Lime Smoothie

Total Prep & Cooking Time: Ten minutes

Yields: Two servings

Nutrition Facts: Calories: 165 | Protein: 2.2g | Carbs: 32.5g | Fat: 4.2g | Fiber: 3.7g

Ingredients

- One cup of ripe mango (frozen, cubed)
- Six cubes of ice
- Half cup of baby spinach leaves
- Two leaves of mint
- Two tsps. of lime juice
- Half cucumber (chopped)
- Three-fourth cup of coconut milk
- One-eighth tsp. of cayenne pepper

Method:

1. Add mango cubes, spinach leaves, and cucumber in a high power blender. Blend until frothy and smooth.
2. Add mint leaves, lime juice, coconut milk, cayenne pepper, and ice cubes. Process the ingredients until smooth.
3. Pour the smoothie in glasses and serve.

Kale, Melon, and Broccoli Smoothie

Total Prep & Cooking Time: Ten minutes

Yields: One serving

Nutrition Facts: Calories: 96.3 | Protein: 2.3g | Carbs: 24.3g | Fat: 1.2g | Fiber: 2.6g

Ingredients

- Eight ounces of honeydew melon
- One handful of kale
- Two ounces of broccoli florets
- One cup of coconut water
- Two sprigs of mint
- Two dates
- Half cup of lime juice
- Eight cubes of ice

Method:

1. Add kale, melon, and broccoli in a food processor. Whizz the ingredients for blending.
2. Add mint leaves and coconut water. Blend again.
3. Add lime juice, dates, and ice cubes. Blend the ingredients until smooth and creamy.
4. Pour the smoothie in a smoothie glass. Enjoy!

Kiwi Spinach Smoothie

Total Prep & Cooking Time: Ten minutes

Yields: Two servings

Nutrition Facts: Calories: 102 | Protein: 3.6g | Carbs: 21.3g | Fat: 2.2g | Fiber: 3.1g

Ingredients

- One kiwi (cut in chunks)
- One banana (cut in chunks)
- One cup of spinach leaves
- Three-fourth cup of almond milk
- One tbsp. of chia seeds
- Four cubes of ice

Method:

1. Add banana, kiwi, and spinach leaves in a blender. Blend the ingredients until smooth.
2. Add chia seeds, ice cubes, and almond milk. Blend again for one minute.
3. Pour the smoothie in serving glasses and serve.

Avocado Smoothie

Total Prep & Cooking Time: Ten minutes

Yields: Two servings

Nutrition Facts: Calories: 345 | Protein: 9.1g | Carbs: 47.8g | Fat: 16.9g | Fiber: 6.7g

Ingredients

- One ripe avocado (halved, pitted)
- One cup of milk
- Half cup of vanilla yogurt
- Eight cubes of ice
- Three tbsps. of honey

Method:

1. Add avocado, vanilla yogurt, and milk in a blender. Blend the ingredients until frothy and smooth.

2. Add honey and ice cubes. Blend the ingredients for making a smooth mixture.

3. Serve immediately.

www.ingramcontent.com/pod-product-compliance
Lightning Source LLC
LaVergne TN
LVHW020412070526
838199LV00054B/3582